Library of
Davidson College

FIGURES OF THE TEXT

PURDUE UNIVERSITY MONOGRAPHS IN ROMANCE LANGUAGES

William M. Whitby, Editor Emeritus
Howard Mancing, General Editor
Enrique Caracciolo-Trejo and Djelal Kadir, Editors for Spanish
Allen G. Wood, Editor for French

Associate Editors

I. French

Max Aprile, Purdue University
Paul Benhamou, Purdue University
Willard Bohn, Illinois State University
Gerard J. Brault, Pennsylvania State University
Germaine Brée, Wake Forest University
Victor Brombert, Princeton University
Ursula Franklin, Grand Valley State College
Floyd F. Gray, University of Michigan
Gerald Herman, University of California, Davis
Michael Issacharoff, University of Western Ontario
Thomas E. Kelly, Purdue University
Milorad R. Margitić, Wake Forest University
Bruce A. Morrissette, University of Chicago
Roy Jay Nelson, University of Michigan
Glyn P. Norton, Williams College
Allan H. Pasco, University of Kansas
David Lee Rubin, University of Virginia
Murray Sachs, Brandeis University
English Showalter, Jr., Rutgers University, Camden
Donald Stone, Jr., Harvard University

II. Spanish

J. B. Avalle-Arce, University of California, Santa Barbara
Rica Brown, M.A., Oxon
Frank P. Casa, University of Michigan
James O. Crosby, Florida International University
Alan D. Deyermond, Westfield College (University of London)
David T. Gies, University of Virginia
Roberto González Echevarría, Yale University
Thomas R. Hart, University of Oregon
David K. Herzberger, University of Connecticut
Floyd F. Merrell, Purdue University
Geoffrey Ribbans, Brown University
Elias L. Rivers, SUNY, Stony Brook
Francisco Ruiz Ramón, Vanderbilt University
J. M. Sobrer, Indiana University
Bruce W. Wardropper, Duke University

Volume 39

Michael Vincent

Figures of the Text

MICHAEL VINCENT

FIGURES OF THE TEXT
Reading and Writing (in) La Fontaine

JOHN BENJAMINS PUBLISHING COMPANY
Amsterdam/Philadelphia

1992

Cover illustration: "Les Deux Pigeons," by J.-J. Grandville; from Jean de La Fontaine, *Fables*, illus. J.-J. Grandville (Paris: Fournier, 1838-40).

Library of Congress Cataloging in Publication Data

Vincent, Michael.
   Figures of the text : reading and writing (in) La Fontaine / Michael Vincent.
   p.   cm. -- (Purdue University monographs in Romance languages, ISSN 0165-8743; v. 39)
Includes bibliographical references and index.
1. La Fontaine, Jean de, 1621-1695--Criticism and interpretation. 2. Books and reading in literature. 3. Reader-response criticism. 4. Authorship in literature. 5. Intertextuality. 6. Allegory. I. Title. II. Series.
PQ1812.V56   1992
841'.4 -- dc20   92-8794
ISBN 90 272 1763 7 (Eur.) / ISBN 1-55619-306-8 (US) (alk. paper) (hardbd.)   CIP
ISBN 90 272 1764 5 (Eur.) / ISBN 1-55619-307-6 (US) (alk. paper) (paperbd.)

© Copyright 1992 - John Benjamins B.V.
No part of this book may be reproduced in any form, by print, photoprint, microfilm, or any other means, without written permission from the publisher.

John Benjamins Publishing Co. · P.O. Box 75577 · 1070 AN Amsterdam · The Netherlands
John Benjamins North America · 821 Bethlehem Pike · Philadelphia, PA 19118 · USA

For Shelley Witman Vincent, my wife and best friend

Table of Contents

Preface .... *ix*
Note on Editions and Abbreviations .... *xiii*

Introduction 1
   Reading La Fontaine 1
   Figures of the Text 8

1. "Hiéroglyphes tout purs": Representations of Writing 11
2. Book, Brain, Body: Citation and the Scene of Reading 21
3. Bodies and Souls: The Intertextual Corpus 41
4. Making the Difference: Textuality and Sexuality 55
5. Inscribing the Voice: Oral Performance and the Written Text 65
6. Description, Representation, and Interpretation 81
7. Reading (through) the Veil 91

Conclusion 109

Notes 115
Works Cited 137
Index 149

Preface

This study has two closely intertwined goals. Of course, this is a book about La Fontaine, that is, about his fables, tales, and prose fiction. As such, it is addressed to all La Fontaine's readers, who will, I hope, find in it something to enrich their reading of La Fontaine. On another level, this book asks questions about what "reading La Fontaine" meant in the seventeenth century, and means today at a three-century remove from the historical moment in which La Fontaine wrote. In some ways, too, this study is an attempt to recapitulate within individual texts of a single distinguished writer the history of writing in the French classical period. Literary readings too solidly embedded in the ideology of voice and presence, our heritage perhaps from this very period, have allowed us to forget other models of reading and writing that are necessarily encoded in the literary product in what I will be calling figures of the text.

The central concern of this study is thus to make explicit within the perspective of a general intertextuality the text's attitude toward itself, and the process of the reader's perception of that attitude. I have thus chosen from La Fontaine's corpus a small number of texts to which I have attached commentaries that depend, of course, on my own perceptions, but also on the history of their reading. Each chapter in this study is a reading of a single text as well as a dialogue with other readings. The practical effect of this choice of critical unity is that theoretical notions are developed as the text under consideration calls for them, within a chapter and across the whole essay. If, as I contend, certain texts by La Fontaine are fully elaborated allegories of reading and writing, then the whole text ought to have its say.

My choice of this particular handful of texts was usually motivated by a critical problem, an anomaly, a certain difficulty in interpretation to which as a (naive?) reader I wanted some resolution. The sexual identity of the two pigeons in "Les Deux Pigeons" in a fable that passes for a love story is a case in point and an example of the kind of critical problem that drew my attention to certain works by La Fontaine. Of course, I believe that these particular texts illustrate something essential about reading and writing in La Fontaine that has not previously been discussed. What I find interesting, however, is how the "detail," the anomaly, the ungrammaticality (in Michael Riffaterre's sense) may serve to figure the whole textual system. My orientation, so to speak, is from the specific—this quotation, this metaphor, this proper name—to the general—citationality, figuration, onomastics. Henri Meschonnic's phrase "l'œuvre dans la figure" (134) may thus be an apt formula for my approach in this study.

While it should be clear that the purpose of this study is not to argue a thesis, or to promote a particular critical doctrine as such, I am nonetheless indebted to the considerable work on reading and writing of the last two decades, especially reader reception theory, theories of intertextuality, and the history and theory of writing, or grammatology. I am, of course, aware that the theorists I cite either in support of my claims, or in opposition to them, often disagree among themselves. Without minimizing important differences, or rehearsing them here, I will in the course of this study display common themes, concerns, attitudes, and approaches in a synthetic work that engages critical writing of all kinds with works by La Fontaine.

The Introduction will serve to place this study within the history of reading La Fontaine, especially that of the last twenty years. It will also explain in more detail what I mean by the title *Figures of the Text*. Chapter 1 is about writing. As the title of the fable under consideration ("Le Fou qui vend la sagesse") indicates, the fable tells the paradoxical story of how a "fool" manages to sell wisdom. A wise man seems to resolve the paradox for one buyer, a "dupe," by reading the configuration of elements composing the story of the fool and his dupe as a "hieroglyphic." This fable thus re-enacts a fundamental problem for contemporary as well as classical language theory, the status of writing with respect to speaking. It is what one might call a fable of the fable, for it stages the origins of the fable genre in heterodox modes of nonphonetic "hieroglyphic" writing, thereby begging to be read as a model of its own production as text.

Chapter 2 is concerned primarily with reading, but also announces the body as scriptural metaphor, the primary theme of the next chapter. If "Démocrite et les Abdéritains" is best known as a philosophical statement of La Fontaine's Epicureanism, it also exhibits features that make it a powerful demonstration of seventeenth-century textuality. The central episode in the

Preface

fable involves a referentially ambiguous but intertextually coherent scene of reading that turns on a corporeal and textual figure, the *labyrinthes d'un cerveau*. At the same time, the fable transcribes textual fragments of all kinds—proverbs, maxims, adages, and allusions—while a pattern of intertextuality by antithesis is established with respect to specific texts by Descartes. The fable closes by putting into (a) question *doxa*'s central maxim: *Vox populi, vox dei*. This chapter studies the relations the text establishes between the citational and doxagraphic modes in which the fable is written and the lessons of the central scene of reading.

Chapter 3 takes on a double fable, "La Laitière et le Pot au lait" and "Le Curé et le Mort" (*Fables* 7.9-10). For three centuries the primary articulation between apologue and moral in the fable genre has sustained intense critical interest. This chapter, however, approaches this division by exploring the originating metaphor of body (apologue) and soul (moral) at work in the text as it grounds the discourse on which the genre and the fables under consideration as instances of that genre are built. The two fables, read as a "double fable," appeal to the founding metaphor of the fable genre by thematizing bodies and souls, telling one more time the story of the inscription of difference, of a privileged interiority (the daydream, the errant soul, the disembodied voice) and parasitical exteriority (the body, the accident). From within this system emerges another, the conjugation of propriety, the proper name, and property.

Chapter 4 discovers that "Les Deux Pigeons" is founded on an anomaly in the sexual roles of the two pigeons. A curious grammatical metamorphosis makes of the traveling pigeon a female character, and therefore allows a "normal," untroubled reading of the fable as a love story.

Chapters 5 and 6 explore La Fontaine's novel, *Les Amours de Psyché et de Cupidon*. Chapter 5 studies the functions of the internal readers and their readings in and of *Psyché*, reflects on the nature of the text that figures these readers reading, and rehearses readerly strategies available for the interpretation of written texts in the seventeenth century. Written texts are, however, not the only sign systems available to *Psyché* or to Poliphile, the fictive author-reader of *Psyché*. In Chapter 6, I continue my reading of *Psyché* in order to consider the relationship between *ekphrasis*, representations of works of art, statuary, tapestries, paintings, and monuments, and the representation of their interpretation in the framing narrative and in the embedded novel itself.

Chapter 7 continues the previous chapter since its text, "Le Tableau" (*Contes* 4.17), purports to be an *ekphrasis*. But "Le Tableau" is an unusual kind of *ekphrasis*. The painting to be described is itself a fiction. What does it mean to cast a vaguely pornographic verse tale in the form of an *ekphrasis*? The representational system elaborated in "Le Tableau" is still more complex, since the tale purportedly describes a painting hidden by curtains. The discourse that is to reveal the painting will, by analogy, be veiled in gauze. Since readers commonly expect to naturalize *ekphrasis* by reconstructing a picture, what happens in the text when this mode of naturalization is withheld, when the *ekphrasis* itself is veiled? What does the poetics of the veil do to the visual model that an *ekphrasis* presumes?

In writing this study I have accumulated enormous debts of every kind. In what follows, I hope to repay in kind some of the intellectual debts I have incurred, but now is the time to acknowledge gratefully the material, practical, and moral support of these individuals and organizations: Ginette Adamson, chair and professor of French at Wichita State University, for her constant encouragement and help at every stage in the elaboration of this project; my colleagues Wilson Baldridge and Servanne Woodward for their insightful comments and thought-provoking conversations; Thomas Blair, Director of the European Studies Association, whose continuing financial support made possible much of the research done in France; Carl Adamson, professor of German at Wichita State University, for hours of technical assistance and practical advice in the preparation of the manuscript; the Wichita State University Research Committee, which provided needed support for my 1987 sabbatical leave in Paris; Joyce Scott, academic vice-president and fellow *dix-septièmiste*, and the Wichita State University Faculty Support Committee for help with the costs of producing this volume; the editors of the *French Review* and *Papers on French Seventeenth-Century Literature* for permission to incorporate previously published material; and PUMRL's anonymous readers, whose interest and attention to every detail have improved this work immeasurably; and finally, Shelley Witman Vincent, my wife and best friend, to whom this work is gratefully dedicated.

Note on Editions and Abbreviations

Throughout this study, quotations from La Fontaine's *Fables choisies mises en vers* and his *Contes et nouvelles en vers* are from the editions established by Georges Couton:

> *Fables choisies mises en vers.* Ed. Georges Couton. Paris: Garnier, 1962. Cited as *Fables* by book and fable.
> *Contes et nouvelles en vers.* Ed. Georges Couton. Paris: Garnier, 1961. Cited as *Contes* by book and tale.

In other references, the edition is indicated as ed. Couton and the appropriate abbreviated title.

Besides the editions noted above, I have made use of the following:

> *Fables.* Ed. Marc Fumaroli. 2 vols. Lettres Françaises. Paris: Imprimerie Nationale, 1985. Cited as ed. Fumaroli, *Fables.*
> *Œuvres complètes: Fables, contes et nouvelles.* Ed. E. Pilon, R. Groos, et J. Schiffrin. Paris: Pléiade-Gallimard, 1954. Cited as Pléiade.
> *Œuvres de J. de la Fontaine.* Ed. Henri Régnier. 12 vols. Les Grands Ecrivains de la France. Paris: Hachette, 1883-92. Cited as ed. Régnier.
> *Les Amours de Psyché et de Cupidon.* In *Œuvres diverses.* Ed. Pierre Clarac. Paris: Pléiade-Gallimard, 1958. Cited as *OD.*

This study was completed before I could take advantage of Jean-Pierre Collinet's new illustrated Pléiade edition of the *Fables* and *Contes* (Jean de La Fontaine. *Œuvres complètes: Fables, contes et nouvelles.* Ed. Jean-Pierre Collinet. Pléiade-Gallimard, 1991). All references in the text and notes to the Pléiade edition refer to the 1958 edition established by Pilon, Groos, and Schiffrin.

In addition, I have used the following abbreviations:

CAIEF   *Cahiers de l'Association Internationale des Etudes Françaises*
FLS   *Foreign Language Studies*
PFSCL   *Papers on French Seventeenth-Century Literature*
PMLA   *Publications of the Modern Language Association*
TWAS   Twayne's World Authors Series

Introduction

READING LA FONTAINE

> [. . .] *il faut laisser / Dans les plus beaux sujets quelque chose à penser.*
>
> La Fontaine
> "Discours à Monsieur le duc
> de la Rochefoucault," *Fables* 10.14

La Fontaine is no longer an easy author. The last twenty years have marked important changes in the way readers approach the act of reading and writing, and critical attitudes about the greatest poet of the French classical period have necessarily evolved along the way. Of course, perspicacious readers were never satisfied with a certain image of La Fontaine that Paul Valéry in his seminal study *Au sujet d'Adonis* evokes in order to denounce:

> Il court sur La Fontaine une rumeur de paresse et de rêverie, un murmure ordinaire d'absence et de distraction perpétuelle, qui nous fait songer sans effort d'un personnage fabuleux, toujours infiniment docile à la plus douce pente de sa durée. (1: 474)

Serious discussion of La Fontaine, it seems, has been marked by a curious imperative; one is obliged to situate the author within a dialectic of apparent facility and real difficulty. This attitude is no doubt encouraged by the *Fables*' statement of their own duplicity: "Les Fables ne sont pas ce qu'elles semblent être" (*Fables* 6.1). André Gide, for example, seems almost surprised to discover the richness of La Fontaine's poetry behind the apparent lightness of touch:

2   Figures of the Text

> Je reprends avec délices, depuis la Fable I, toutes les fables de La Fontaine. Je ne vois pas trop de quelle qualité l'on pourrait dire qu'il ne fasse pas preuve. Celui qui sait bien voir peut y trouver trace de tout; mais il faut un œil averti, tant la touche, souvent, est légère. C'est un miracle de culture. Sage comme Montaigne; sensible comme Mozart. (10)

Writing on the occasion of La Fontaine's three hundred fiftieth birthday, Jacques Gaucheron characterized perfectly this pattern of reader reception that runs through much critical writing on La Fontaine:

> On a pu croire qu'une lecture enjouée suffisait à faire le tour de son œuvre, et qu'une fable une fois lue, avait livré ses secrets un peu fades et distillé son charme alangui. Certains lecteurs peuvent penser que la recherche des significations est de trop de poids sur cette poésie légère. (6)

As readers of all kinds become increasingly convinced of the necessary connection between the act of reading a text and specular reflection on reading as such, fewer today would doubt that the "papillon du Parnasse" could survive the presumably heavy artillery of literary theory, even when "theory" is taken to mean a thesis to be proved or a system to be illustrated.[1] Jonathan Culler has, however, pointed to the recent emergence of a new genre, that, for lack of another term, he calls "theory," too (*On Deconstruction* 8-9). Remaining closer to the word's etymological roots in the Greek *theoria* ("viewing, contemplation, speculation"), this "theory" is not strictly speaking "literary theory," since the object of study is not necessarily literature, nor is it "philosophy" in the current sense of the term. It is not "literature" either, although it is often concerned with its own fictionality. By "theory" I will mean something very close to the class of intermediate and mediating discourse to which Culler points. If grand theory's goal is to answer questions, that is, to put an end to theory by blocking in advance other critical moves, I would rather keep the game going through a critical examination of and a reflection on the assumptions that condition reading and writing. Theory in this sense is at the heart of the modern literary experience and cannot be divorced from the production or reception of texts.

It is a tribute to the diversity and richness of La Fontaine's poetry that some of his readers still find in his work the medium through which theory is thought. They have certainly made contributions to the kind of theory Culler has described. As a preamble to this study, I would like to acknowledge the poet's fortunes in the (post-)modern world and thereby situate this essay within the critical and theoretical ambience that has nourished it and to which it aspires to contribute.[2]

The work of Michel Serres stands as an exemplary case. In *Le Parasite*, for example, Serres rethinks communication theory through La Fontaine's fables. Serres's commentaries on La Fontaine are not mere examples convenient to an argument that logically precedes the necessity of choosing an illustration; they are dialogues with the text in which the fable and "theory" mutually nourish each other. A similar procedure informs Louis Marin's *Le Récit est un piège*, in which he discovers (or invents) in La Fontaine, Racine, Perrault, and others a figure (the *récit* as trap) without which it is no longer possible to think about seventeenth-century French literature. The theoretical power of Marin's discovery has only begun to be tapped, no doubt because traps are no longer a part of the world of people who are inclined to write books about seventeenth-century French literature.[3]

While La Fontaine's modern compatriots expand his work in ever more interesting ways, scholars on this side of the Atlantic, proceeding from somewhat different cultural and intellectual presuppositions, continue to find in La Fontaine a source of pleasure and instruction. It would be inaccurate to suggest that American students of La Fontaine constitute anything like a distinct school of thought. However, as a group they display features common to their interpretive community. Despite local differences, most rely on close textual readings that insist on the double interplay of text and reflection on the text, or "theory" as I have tried to define it above.

Some of the most interesting recent work on La Fontaine in North America has turned on the question of irony, one of the slipperiest notions available to critic or reader, and not incidentally, one of the essential critical strategies of the New Criticism. Irony occasioned the fruitful exchange between Susan Tiefenbrun and Jules Brody, published in *Papers on French Seventeenth-Century Literature*. The dialogue between a late structuralist formalism built on an antiphrastic, binary pattern and a kind of textual, or intertextual, reading virtually reset the agenda for La Fontaine studies. Writing about La Fontaine will now entail rehearsing the paradigmatic shift implicit in these two critics' critical difference. David Lee Rubin extended the labyrinthine complexities of La Fontaine's irony in a brilliantly provocative article on "double irony," first defined by D. C. Muecke and later refined by Wayne C. Booth. I would certainly endorse Rubin's contention that "to discover the double ironist's meaning is a tortuous process" (202), especially when at least one variety permits the reader to undermine the text's own ironic position. Rubin's convincing analyses of examples of double irony in La Fontaine lead us to wonder whether indeed irony at the expense of irony can ever be resolved through the application of an antiphrastic model.

Richard Danner's recent *Patterns of Irony*, an extensive and theoretically ambitious exploration of La Fontaine's fables, re-examines the question of irony in La Fontaine, especially in the structural, stylistic, and thematic aspects of the *Fables*. Danner succeeds in demonstrating through his careful close readings the range and complexity of La Fontaine's ironic vision. At the same time, the theory of irony is enriched through its contact with La Fontaine in Danner. The conclusion to this study will review Danner's program of inquiry into the *Fables* with respect to what this study hopes to have achieved and what remains to be investigated.

This study, oddly perhaps, given my considerable debt to these theorists of irony in La Fontaine, has little to say about irony as such. Taking my cue from Jules Brody's framing of the situation, I have preferred to think in terms of a poetics of doubleness and duplicity, a kind of essential irony:

[T]he irony, or the poetry of doubleness and duplicity, has its roots [. . .] in the deconstruction of rhetorical modes, in the weaving together of opaque discursive, previously invented lexical elements in a poetic fabric. (Brody, "Irony" 87)

My interest in doubleness and duplicity in La Fontaine is shared by Patrick Dandrey, who, by continuing the work of Jean-Pierre Collinet on "double fables" (*Le Monde littéraire* 163), has studied in considerable depth techniques of *dédoublement* in La Fontaine, notably in his "La Fable double de l'*Horoscope*: Une Poétique implicite de La Fontaine."

The common means of interrogation in each of the chapters that constitute this study is the analysis of procedures of reception of the literary work. For this approach, I implicitly draw on the seminal work of Hans Robert Jauss, Wolfgang Iser, and Michael Riffaterre. The notion of a reader itself remains highly problematical. What reader, or readers, are we talking about? La Fontaine's contemporaries, or ours? The *naïf* who takes the ironic for the serious? The *faux naïf* whose pleasure it is to imagine the *naïf* taken in? The "implied reader," or merely another version of myself? In his influential essay on "The Poetic Text within the Change of Horizons of Reading" in *Toward an Aesthetic of Reception*, Hans Robert Jauss doubles the reader in his critical text in a way that attempts to avoid these pitfalls for a theory of reader reception:

> [. . .] I have not fabricated something like a "naive reader," but have rather transposed myself into the role of a reader with the educational horizon of our contemporary present. The role of this historical reader should presuppose that one is experienced with lyrics, but that one can initially suspend one's literary historical or linguistic competence, and put in its place the capacity occasionally to wonder during the course of the reading, and to express this wonder in the form of questions. Beside this historical reader from 1979, I have placed a commentator with scholarly competence, who deepens the aesthetic impressions of the reader whose understanding takes the form of pleasure, and who refers back to the text's structures of effect as much as possible. (144)

Jauss even takes the precaution of distinguishing typographically between the discourse of the reader who suspends certain of his acquired competencies and that of the scholar who comments on the text and on the responses of the "first" reader. Jauss's "reader" is thus in some respects punctuation, or "writing" in some of the senses Jacques Derrida has given to the term. What I will be calling the reader in this study is this self-doubling "I," without the literary signs of Jauss's fictive dialogue. "The writer's audience is always a fiction" (Ong 53). So am I. In this respect, I am very close to the position taken by Patrick Dandrey. Writing on *Psyché*, Dandrey has pointed out to what extent La Fontaine's implied reader is already necessarily doubled:

> Il y a là comme un dédoublement de la fonction réceptrice: le destinataire, c'est d'un côté, l'auditeur ou le lecteur de l'ouvrage, individualisé, pourvu d'une culture et d'une information suffisantes, capable de prendre ses distances, de formuler des critiques—le *docte*; et puis, d'un autre côté, c'est le public, collectif, abstrait, produit ou seulement visé et défini par l'œuvre même comme "transhistorique" et "transindividuel" [. . .] non plus le lecteur docte, mais l'impossible idéal honnête homme du présent et de l'avenir. ("Stratégie" 833)

La Fontaine's works thus deliberately form their reader, invent the reader in the text, and solicit one's willing identification with that reader, even when the reader must feel the ricochet of "double irony" at his own expense. As Jean-Pierre Collinet put it in his essay on "L'Art de lire selon La Fontaine":

"L'art du conteur et du fabuliste se fonde sur une analyse finement originale des moyens propres à circonvenir celui qui lit" (92). John D. Lyons's article on "Author and Reader in the *Fables*" fully demonstrates the extent to which La Fontaine engages with his reader in the text. Lyons's central thesis can in some ways stand as a program for one aspect of this study:

> In many fables the author clearly attempts to create a specifically literary consciousness of the fable's existence as language and as form, to keep the reader in a state of constant awareness of the text as a text, and even to make the act and moment of creation of the work the true focus of the reader's attention. Far from encouraging us to forget the artificiality and formal nature of the fable, La Fontaine continuously violates the narrative or mimetic space of the poem with indications of its boundaries, foundations, and origin. (Lyons, "Author and Reader" 59)

Another intriguing feature of La Fontaine's poetry for the modern reader is the resistance it sometimes raises to our contemporary modes and habits of reading. Contemporary critical taste often runs toward the perception of difficulty in poetry. Thematic, stylistic, philological, or narrative anomalies and discontinuities provoke the reader, presumably desirous of order, to look for unity on another level of coherence. Jules Brody's remarks are absolutely pertinent for modern readers of La Fontaine:

> For the serious reader, the problem is always the same: to find some break in the flow of the text, some palpable sign of a hidden complexity, some ungrammaticality to tell us that everything is really *not* alright after all. Where, so we ask, is the catachresis that will lead us to the hypogram? ("La Fontaine" 144-45)

Although, as I will show, there is no lack of hidden complexities in La Fontaine's poetry, it does often seem to be La Fontaine's smoothness, his Horatian *suavitas* (Spitzer, "L'Art de la transition"), that becomes oddly problematic for the modern reader.

Literary discourse of any kind is highly allusive. La Fontaine's work is not the exception but the paragon, as André Gide quickly discovered when he began to reread the fables he thought he knew. Meaning emerges in the explicit or implicit comparison with other literary texts, either by repetition, imitation, or contradiction. Intertextuality is thus the heart of the experience of the text. In this respect I follow Michael Riffaterre's account of the reader's perception and actualization of the intertext, elaborated in many books and articles, but in its most closely argued form in his *Semiotics of Poetry*. Pierre Malandain, in his *Fable et l'intertexte,* was the first to apply rigorously and extensively the notion of intertextuality to La Fontaine's *Fables*. His reading of no fewer than sixty-six fables amply demonstrates the formal means at the poet's disposal for embedding texts within texts, for creating spaces of textual exchange. Jules Brody's intertextual reading of "Les Vautours et les Pigeons" ("La Fontaine") brilliantly confirms the interest of this approach to La Fontaine.

What remains now to be said about La Fontaine? Three centuries of readers, writers, critics, and commentators have done their work very well. They have taken to heart the plowman's advice to his sons, and perhaps an author's advice to his readers and critics:

> Creusez, fouillez, bêchez; ne laissez nulle place
> Où la main ne passe et repasse.
> ("Le Laboureur et ses Enfants," *Fables* 5.9)

Like the plowman's sons, La Fontaine's readers have left their field richer for their work, their own investment in "La Fontaine," while leaving behind the traces of their interrogation in the form of innumerable glosses and interpretations academic, pedagogic, philosophical, philological, historical, and even scientific. The text we still call a "La Fontaine fable" is no longer what it was when its author, working and reworking material inherited from a thousand sources, first put pen to paper. Our task, the one that now seems to impose itself with the recognition of the profound intertextuality of any literary work, is to take account of the countless inscriptions, the more or less readable traces that compose our classic texts. There is no need to pretend to scrape away the accretions of all past readings in order to peer through the textual palimpsest to the first (that is, true) writing, waiting there like the plowman's treasure. What is needed perhaps at this late date is a gloss not too taken with its own innocence, a sounding through the multiple textual levels that compose a La Fontaine fable or tale.

8   Figures of the Text

FIGURES OF THE TEXT

> *The trope which any text proposes for itself*
> *contains its unholy ghost*[.]
> William Gass
> *Habitations of the World*

    One of the principal assumptions I will be testing in this study is, as the title indicates, the notion of the text itself, and its figuration in La Fontaine's fables, prose fiction, and tales. In her excellent "Texte, Textus, Hyphos," Marie-Rose Logan ranks the word and notion *text* among the "quelques dizaines de mots essentiels dont l'ensemble constitue le bien commun de l'ensemble des langues occidentales" (69).[4] Her survey of the word and notion begins, obligatorily, with the Greeks represented by Longinus, and the Romans represented by Cicero, Quintilian, and Ovid, and arrives as quickly as possible at Roland Barthes, the main subject of her essay. While the intervening millenia fall outside the scope of her article, a question arises from within the gap in her survey: What of the medieval, Renaissance, seventeenth-century, or Enlightenment "text," to propose a program Lagarde or Michard would respect? I will be attempting a provisional response for La Fontaine by exploring what I find to be special moments in La Fontaine's corpus in which the interplay of texts reading texts reveals itself in a figure of the process of textual production. As resolutely modern as this project may seem, I do not believe it is in any sense anachronistic. If the language we must use in discussing the essential intertextuality and its specular display in La Fontaine is modern, the phenomenon, I will be showing, is not; it may very well be imposed by the practice of writing itself. One should not, however, expect classical and modern notions of textuality to be identical. Their differences and similarities constitute a major theme of this study.[5]

    In this kind of interrogation, one inevitably risks begging the question, finding the answer because it is already implied in the question.[6] As Logan points out (73), Barthes himself at first seemed to endow *text* with axiomatic connotations. Later in *Le Plaisir du texte* (1973), he radically displaces what had been his founding metaphor and premise, and demonstrates how to avoid begging the question of the text. As point of departure and as illustration of what I mean by figure of the text, I propose at the outset of this study two possible figures of the text suggested by Barthes in his reading of the founding metaphor of modern textuality:

Introduction 9

Texte veut dire *Tissu*; mais alors que jusqu'ici on a toujours pris ce tissu pour un produit, un voile tout fait, derrière lequel se tient, plus ou moins caché, le sens (la vérité), nous accentuons maintenant, dans le tissu, l'idée générative que le texte se fait, se travaille à travers un entrelacs perpétuel; perdu dans ce tissu—cette texture—le sujet s'y défait, telle une araignée qui se dissoudrait elle-même dans les sécrétions constructives de sa toile. Si nous aimions les néologismes, nous pourrions, en effet, définir la théorie du texte comme une *hyphologie* (*hyphos*, c'est le tissu et la toile d'araignée). (*Le Plaisir du texte* 101-02)

This imagery is bound to strike the fancy of La Fontaine's admirers, since it constitutes a fable of the text, complete with animal "character" (the spider), plot (the spider's dissolving in her own secretions), an allegorical (moral?) sense (the loss of the subject in writing), and even a discreet nod to classical mythology (the Arachne legend).[7] Barthes here illustrates a fundamental insight in what has come to be called poststructural criticism, namely, that in Jules Brody's words, "our critical vocabularies, like all language, are hopelessly, helplessly metaphoric before they are either concrete or abstract" ("Irony" 80-81). The term *text* is, of course, itself a catachresis, a term inevitably perceived as a metaphor for which no "proper" term exists. Modern theories of the text cannot do without *texte veut dire tissu* any more than certain schools of literary studies can do without their fluid metaphors (sources and inspiration); or linguistics, its particular geography (verticality of the paradigmatic; horizontality of the syntagmatic). If the text were not a *tissu*, what else could it be? All that seems to remain is to rehearse the unraveling of *text*'s etymology.[8] One aspect of this study is to discover what figures of reading and writing seemed in this way essential to La Fontaine as examples of seventeenth-century textuality at play.

In the passage quoted above, Barthes suggests one possibility, common at least in part, to the seventeenth and twentieth centuries, that I will explore more fully in my final chapter, "Reading (through) the Veil." If, at a certain distance, the veil seems a fair figure of classical textuality, closer readings reveal that the veil itself has a texture. My task will be to maintain simultaneously both perspectives within the problematic of the text by showing that, as La Fontaine's texts reflect on their own reading and writing, the double aspect of Barthes's figure, the text as veil and the text as "entrelacs perpétuel," is displayed. This study is thus inscribed somewhere between Barthes's classical "toujours" and "maintenant."

The vocation of this study, then, is to conjugate a theory of reading, of reception and perception, and a theory of textual production by drawing attention particularly to those aspects of the text that figure writing and reading: scenes of reading; other modes of writing (emblematics, hieroglyphics, and their *mise en scène*); proper names; forms of intertextuality and citationality (proverbs, maxims, allusions); the relation of represented orality to textuality, of textuality to corporeality, of textuality to the visual arts; inscriptions and epitaphs; and the archaeology of textual figures (labyrinths, hieroglyphics, textiles, veils).

1
"Hiéroglyphes tout purs": Representations of Writing

"Le Fou qui vend la sagesse"

"Le Fou qui vend la sagesse" (*Fables* 9.8) tells the paradoxical story of how a "fou" manages to sell the wisdom or good sense he cannot be said to possess:

> Un Fol allait criant par tous les carrefours
> Qu'il vendait la Sagesse; et les mortels crédules
> De courir à l'achat: [...]

The credulous for their money get a performance ("force grimaces"), a slap in the face, and a rope. Consumer reaction to this display is mixed. One buyer, no doubt the craziest of the lot, takes his case to a wise man, a "sage," for interpretation. The *sage* without hesitation replies: "Ce sont ici hiéroglyphes tout purs." He then goes on to explain that the story does indeed have an important sense and that the *fou* therefore did sell him what he claimed:

> Les gens bien conseillés, et qui voudront bien faire,
> Entre eux et les gens fous mettront pour l'ordinaire
> La longueur de ce fil; sinon je les tiens sûrs
>   De quelque semblable caresse.
> Vous n'êtes point trompé: ce fou vend la sagesse.

This fable contains more than one good lesson, as La Fontaine has had the occasion to remind us in other contexts. Marc Soriano, for example, takes this fable as a point of departure for a study of "folie" in La Fontaine's fables and finds that *folie* constitutes a fundamental articulation in the *Fables* (6).

Composed near the historical beginnings of the modern discourse on insanity, La Fontaine's *histoires de fous* are interesting in an archaeological sense. Soriano brilliantly develops this aspect of the *Fables* by revealing the curious interdependence of what everyone knows to be opposite and contradictory behaviors.[1] At the end of the fable, *sagesse* is still defined as *sagesse*, and *folie* still *folie*, and in this sense nothing has changed. Nothing, but that in this fable at least, one might become the other.

In this chapter, I would like to circumvent the broader question of wisdom and folly and their paradoxical relationship in this fable in order to concentrate on the wise man's reading of what he calls "pure hieroglyphics," that is, on a peculiar act of interpretation that invests the *histoire de fou* with a meaning. I will be arguing that this fable re-enacts a fundamental problem for contemporary as well as classical language theory, the status of writing with respect to speaking.[2] This fable allegorizes the essential intertextuality of the fable genre by thematizing the passage from represented action in the "world" to a text, a "hieroglyphic," which, paradoxically, must be prior to the action it purports to represent. It is what one might call a fable of the fable in that it begs to be read as a model of its own production as text.

Like most of La Fontaine's fables, this fable is formally divided into the moral, which in this instance serves as exordium, and the apologue proper. The title is of the sort that might easily serve as the *mot* for an emblem. The apologue itself takes place in two moments, each of which represents an act of communication that could be fruitfully analyzed according to Jakobson's well-tested communication model.[3] In the first moment, the *fou*, apparently the "speaking" subject of his discourse, attempts to communicate directly to credulous buyers a message that, under the circumstances, may or may not have a meaning. The contact between subject and receiver of the message depends on their physical proximity for the receiver to observe the faces the *fou* makes, and for the transmission of the slap on the face and the rope:

> On essuyait forces grimaces;
> Puis on avait pour son argent,
> Avec un bon soufflet un fil long de deux brasses.

This first scene in which this curious message is transmitted depends on models of oral communication for its narrative coherence, although not a word is in fact spoken. A "present" moment with respect to time and place has been clearly established, and a contact with the other has been offered within a network of traditionally recognized relations, namely buying and selling.

"Hiéroglyphes tout purs"

There is, however, a problem. As Jacques Derrida has amply demonstrated, the discourse of wisdom in Western thought depends precisely on the myth of immediacy, on the unmediated exchange of words in which the materiality of the signifier, its density and opacity, needs to be forgotten. In this fable, the signifiers are themselves objects that seem to stand for words in somewhat the same way as words were thought to stand for things. For educated seventeenth-century readers, this fable might very likely recall the story of Darius and the Scythians recounted by Herodotus (2.16). The Scythians send the king of the Persians a bird, a mouse, a frog, and five arrows. Their gift was read to mean "unless you turn into a bird that flies in the air, a mouse to burrow into the earth, or a frog to hide in the waters, you will not escape our arrows." This combination of objects is already a kind of writing in which the "sign" is not distinguished from the referent (Kristeva, *Langages* 30). It is interesting to note at this point that the slap on the face curiously takes on some of the material durability of the rope while the *fou*'s *grimaces* seem to evaporate like words into the air. (After all, *grimaces* do have a coded meaning; they are the traditional signs of *folie* of one sort or another.) The narrator advises the buyer of "wisdom" to go away "sans rien dire *avec* son soufflet et son fil." Later, the dupe goes to consult the sage "Du fil et du soufflet pourtant embarrassé." The syllepsis leaves two meanings open for *embarrassé*, "embarrassed" or "physically weighted down." The slap and the rope have acquired the same level of materiality. However, unlike the Scythians' message to Darius, no message can be said to be communicated by the *fou* to his dupe first of all because of the heavy doubt placed on the "speaker's" performative capacities. The Scythians' message was interpretable because of an implied intent to communicate a message; the *fou* is judged incapable of clear intent. The Scythians' message was framed by situation (arrows => war) and a certain redundancy in the code (mouse, bird, fish => timorousness leading to flight). Nothing in the situation or in the code allows easy decipherment of the *fou*'s message. The *fou*'s performance does, nevertheless, parody authentic acts of communication, since, all else being equal, the speech act of wisdom transmission has been performed according to model.

In a second moment, a buyer of wisdom, a "dupe" according to the narrator, tells his story to the wise man, who then proceeds to the interpretation with the self-assurance that is no doubt the sign of another kind of *folie*:

> Un des dupes un jour alla trouver un sage,
>   Qui, sans hésiter davantage,
> Lui dit: Ce sont ici hiéroglyphes tout purs.

The rather unexpected use of an erudite term like *hieroglyphic* raises a number of interesting questions. Of course, a sage might be expected to speak a bit pedantically just as a *fou* might be expected to act insanely. *Stultus stulta loquitur* (Erasmus, *Adages*). On another level, the fable certainly parodies a universal constant of literary criticism; critics will always make texts say what the author could never have meant. However, for the sake of the argument, let us take the sage perfectly seriously. What might it mean for the dupe's story to be read as a hieroglyphic? The reader is alerted to the possibility that something other than folly and wisdom are at issue in this fable, since the paradox proposed in the title depends entirely on the sage's ability to read the dupe's story as a figure carrying a mysterious truth hidden from the general public but certainly accessible to the wise man. While it would not be helpful to restrict the fable to an overly rigorous definition, it is of considerable interest to note the semantic range and weight of the term as it was understood by the literate public in the late seventeenth century.[4]

The hieroglyphic, narrowly understood as a particular form of Egyptian writing, has done long and distinguished duty as a literary symbol from the Renaissance to modern times (Dieckmann). The discovery of hieroglyphics on Egyptian obelisks imported to Rome may be considered the historical event that opened the debate on writing that raged throughout the seventeenth century (Compagnon 259-60). Before Champollion actually succeeded in deciphering them, they were largely considered to be a symbolic mode of expression that contained moral or religious truths accessible to the erudite. The discovery in 1419 of Horapollo's *Hieroglyphica*, considered the key to the symbolic interpretation of hieroglyphics, set the fashion for the Renaissance (David 22). This tradition touched La Fontaine directly and closely. One of the most prestigious works in the idealized "Egyptian" tradition, Francesco Colonna's *Hypnerotomachia Poliphili* (Venice, 1499) was an important source for La Fontaine's *Psyché* (Blunt). I must, of course, carefully distinguish between two historical moments in the conception of the hieroglyphic. For Derrida and disciples, grammatology's interest in hieroglyphics is linked to their double nature as phonetic *and* as ideogrammatic writing. Before Champollion and Warburton, that is, from the time of their discovery through the Enlightenment, they were considered uniquely ideogrammatic. However, their contamination by rebuses in the practice of constructing new hieroglyphics (as distinct from deciphering, or pretending to decipher, Egyptian hieroglyphics) did indeed bring them closer to the "modern" notion.

"Hiéroglyphes tout purs"

There is good reason to believe that by extension the term *hieroglyphic* as it was commonly used in the French seventeenth century included all nonalphabetic modes of signifying inscription as practiced in the seventeenth century and the Renaissance. I will let the complete title of César Ripa's *Iconologia* in Jean Baudoin's 1644 translation reveal the range of the term and the importance of this mode of signification:

> *Iconologie ou explication nouvelle de plusieurs images, emblèmes et autres figures hiéroglyphiques des Vertus, des Arts, des Sciences, des causes naturelles, des humeurs différentes et de passions humaines. Œuvre augmentée d'une seconde partie, nécessaire à toutes sortes d'esprits et particulièrement à ceux qui aspirent à être ou sont en effet orateurs, poètes, sculpteurs, peintres, ingénieurs, auteurs de médailles, de devises, de ballets et de poèmes dramatiques, tirés des recherches de César Ripa, moralisées par J. Baudoin.*[5]

The preface to Gilles Corrozet's *Hecatomgraphie* (1540) establishes even more closely the link between the hieroglyphic and what moderns would more likely consider a branch of the decorative arts:

> Ce livret qui contient cent Emblèmes
> Authoritez, Sentences, Apophtegmes
> Des biens lettrés, comme Plutarque et aultres,
> Et toutefois, il y a des nostres
> Grande quantité, aussi de nos amys [...]
> Chacune histoire est d'image illustrée
> Affin que soit plus clairement monstrée
> L'invention et la rendre authentique,
> Qu'on peut nommer *lettre hiérogliphique*
> Comme jadis faisaient les anciens
> Et entre tous les Vieux Egyptiens,
> Qui dénotaient vice ou vertu honneste
> Par ung oiseau, un poisson, une beste [...]
> Aussy pourront ymagers et tailleurs,
> Painctres, brodeurs, orfèvres, émailleurs
> Prendre en ce livre aulcune fantasie
> Comme ils feraient d'une tapisserie.
>
> (Qtd. in Couton, *Poétique* 9)

For Baudoin, the modern emblem owes its origins to hieroglyphic writing:

> Il ne faut pas s'étonner, si telles figures servaient autrefois de caractères aux Egyptiens, comme elles servent encore aujourd'hui à la plupart des nations du nouveau monde. Et d'autant que les actions vertueuses étaient ordinairement signifiées par ces caractères hiéroglyphiques, c'était la coutume aussi de les appeler mystérieux at sacrés. A leur imitation ont été inventé les emblèmes [. . .]. (*Recueil d'emblèmes divers* vol. 1, preface [np].)

It is clear that for Baudoin and Corrozet allegorical images and emblems were varieties of *figures hiéroglyphiques*. The second edition of the *Dictionnaire de l'Académie* even defines the emblem as an "espèce de figure hiéroglyphique qui est d'ordinaire accompagné de quelques paroles sententieuses." Daniel S. Russell, in his remarkable study on emblems, notes in this definition a sign of the emblem's generic specificity at this late date (108). The Jesuit Claude-François Ménestrier, whose name will reappear several times in this study, as specialist in figures of all sorts, was himself extraordinarily conscientious in distinguishing, that is, in finding or inventing differences, between emblems, hieroglyphics, *devises*, and "symbols." This dictionary definition would indicate that his distinctions were not so finely traced in the minds of his contemporaries. Russell points out the difficulty in isolating the emblem from other similar practices. "In fact, it was rather more an attitude, towards visual and even literary art [. . .]" (103).

It seems likely that the fable's *hiéroglyphes tout purs* in this wider acceptation alludes to the immense corpus of emblems, devices, and blasons that so delighted the seventeenth century and whose importance for literary studies, the theory of language, and the text is only now being rediscovered. In his *Poétique de La Fontaine*, Georges Couton convincingly demonstrates the literary relationship between the structure of the emblem and the structure of the fable and posits emblematic sources, or *contaminatio* from emblematic sources, for some of the fables. He concedes, however, that La Fontaine, who willingly pays his literary debts to Aesop, Phaedrus, or Pilpay, never names an author of emblems or even mentions the word *emblem* (16). In a later article, Couton himself almost borrows Baudoin's widely inclusive term *hiéroglyphe* to designate the second language of allegory common to both the plastic and verbal arts, although he finally prefers the more modern *ideogram* ("Réapprendre" 84). If the connection is made between Couton's two interrogations of other modes of writing in seventeenth-century texts (which to my knowledge Couton never made), then "Le Fou qui vend la sagesse" may very well contain the "missing" reference to the emblematic tradition that Couton has proved so important for the understanding of La Fontaine's poetics. Unfortunately for this line of inquiry, La Fontaine's sole reference to this tradition in the *Fables* is embedded in a paradoxical and ironic discourse that does not allow for easy conclusions about the poet's attitude toward that tradition. If it is impossible, based solely on the evidence of "Le Fou qui vend la sagesse," to evaluate La Fontaine's opinion of this peculiar art form, it is nonetheless true that this fable stages a scene that presupposes a generalized form of hieroglyphic writing in Baudoin's sense of the word. The fable's sage may be truly wise, or crazier than the *fou*, but his particular form of wisdom, or folly, is explicitly linked to the hieroglyphic mode of reading and writing current in La Fontaine's day.

***

La Fontaine's tale leaves out a crucial step in the succession of events that will create meaning out of madness. The dupe's act of recounting his story to the sage is omitted from the fable, no doubt for reasons of narrative economy. Thus, from the reader's point of view, the fable's first telling of the incident in the narratorial voice is identical or at least coterminous with the dupe's omitted *récit*. For the sage-interpreter, the story told by the dupe does constitute a message, but, contrary to what the reader of the fable might have initially assumed, the message does not reside in the tokens of exchange (*grimaces, soufflet, fil*). These tokens do not stand for things, nor do they stand for words, even though the scene in which they are transmitted parodies a scene of speaking and reception. The message must be read as a "written" text, a configuration, or rather a re-configuration, of elements which includes the *fou* and the dupe as signifiers of the same nature as the rope, the slap, and the *fou*'s grimaces.

The "message," as revealed by the sage, could not have been communicated in the first scene, the scene of its representation, because the contact between speaker and receiver presupposed a verbal model of communication based on the immediate apprehension of a message between subjects in which the signifiers are effaced in favor of the signified. The scene can only be truly understood at a distance, at a point where the constituent elements can be understood as inscriptions in the world, as a hieroglyphic, a pictogram in which spatial disposition takes the place of syntax. Since the meaning of the tale cannot be guaranteed by reference to the *fou*'s intention to communicate a message, it can only be a function of this configuration of elements, independent of any "authorial" intention. The first scene was undecipherable less because of the obscurity of the code than because it was not yet a text. The second scene, the scene of interpretation, reconstitutes the first as text and thereby renders it interpretable. This is possible only on condition that the *fou* and his customer may themselves be counted as signifiers rather than as subject and receiver of a potentially meaningful message. The *fou* and the dupe are now truly "characters" in many of the senses given this term. They are marks, inscriptions, hieroglyphics; they are immutable, eternal essences incapable of change or development. They are their names. The scene in which these "characters" appear, which the reader might take for representation of an action in the world, a sequential ordering of events in time, has been displaced by a timeless and authorless, but now finally meaningful, figure. It is noteworthy that in La Fontaine's source (Abstemius, fable 185) the *fou* himself immediately provides the interpretation of his behavior along with the punch and the rope (ed. Couton, *Fables* 502n.). In this fable, the *fou*'s words gloss his actions in a way that is situationally paradoxical but theoretically unproblematic. La Fontaine's rewriting of the fable divides the single scene into two narrative moments of enactment and interpretation, divides Abstemius's *fou*'s role into two, *fou* and *sage*, and thereby displays the underlying tension between the narration of represented action in the world and its subsequent recomposition as "hieroglyphic" in this fable.

As we have seen, the fable of "Le Fou qui vend la sagesse" rehearses the inner workings of a mode of reading and writing current in western Europe from the Renaissance through the seventeenth century. La Fontaine's mention of a "pure hieroglyphic" is thus entirely in keeping with his age's fascination with pictorial modes of writing that silently double the verbal text.[6] I will take up the relation of picture to language in two chapters, one devoted to La Fontaine's novel *Les Amours de Psyché et de Cupidon*, the other to his tale "Le Tableau." In the emblem, of course, these two modes of writing were physically juxtaposed on the page in a way that was intended to create a significant unity of greater depth than either "text" alone. The most common metaphor for the particular relationship of the verbal text to the pictorial text was the soul and the body, the same metaphor that La Fontaine uses to explain the relationship between the fable and its moral. I will be exploring the fuller implications of this metaphor in Chapter 3.

Of course, the theoretical possibility of transforming image into language and language into image without embarrassing residue was never seriously doubted even to the point that the verbal description of an absent or nonexistent picture could fulfill the structural requirements of the emblem genre. In his *Art des emblèmes* (1662; 1684), Claude-François Ménestrier, one of the most perspicacious theorists of the emblem, shows, for example, how La Fontaine's "Deux Mulets" (*Fables* 1.4) and "L'Astrologue qui se laisse tomber dans un puits" (*Fables* 2.13) could be read as emblems (Couton, *Poétique* 6-7). Ménestrier thus provides a coherent and contemporary model of a mode of reading that could be usefully applied to "Le Fou." This model is all the more precious for its rarity in the seventeenth century. Couton's work with Ménestrier and La Fontaine, together with Margaret M. McGowan's elaborations of Couton's approach, show how the fable itself is clearly linked to the emblematic tradition, although neither cites "Le Fou" specifically in this context. The *fou* with his contorted faces, rope, and aggressive behavior could be a character out of the *Iconologia*; the paradoxical title might serve as the motto and the sage's explanation, the emblem's explanatory text.

On another level, "Le Fou" is a practical demonstration of how an emblem is written and read. It provides another model of reading and writing by allegorizing what Daniel S. Russell has called the "emblematic process." Russell adapts Genette's adaptation of Lévi-Strauss's influential distinction between the *ingénieur* and the *bricoleur* in order to find that the emblematist is a pure *bricoleur*:

> [T]he emblematist tended to disassemble some cultural edifice, some "sous-ensemble de la culture" [Lévi-Strauss, *La Pensée sauvage* 29], or take fragments left over from earlier disintegrations or de-constructions, and then reassemble some parts of the original edifice in new or modified configurations. The emblematist is, then, more nearly a pure *bricoleur* than the critic, and hence, he is even more radically opposed to the "artist" than the critic is. (Russell 175)

La Fontaine's fable shows the *bricoleur* at work as the sage disassembles the dupe's narrative, reorders the fragments drained of all meanings they might have had, and declares the new configuration to be "pure hieroglyphics." This is why in La Fontaine's version of the story the *fou* could not be cast as the interpreter of the message, and why the sage could not be present at the original scene. The sage as emblematist-*bricoleur* can only work on a previously textualized artifact. In this fable, reading is, as Antoine Compagnon put it, an invention of emblems (270).

Despite the relative clarity with which this fable allegorizes the concomitant practices of reading and writing, no one would dream of considering this fable a model for reading that could be applied to other fables. It should not, however, be considered merely as an *histoire de fou*, or even as an antimodel, a model of how not to read. It seems rather an etiological myth, an explanatory tale of origins, a fable that tells how there came to be hieroglyphics. This fable, it seems to me, is best read as the re-enactment, the *mise en scène* of the prehistory of the hieroglyphic (or emblematic) mode of reading and writing. La Fontaine's sage reads/writes his hieroglyphic by fixing once and for all each of the elements found in the dupe's tale into a meaningful configuration. But meaning is expensive. The origin of the message discovered in the dupe's tale, the notion of an intending author, and the subjectivity of the human "characters" must be sacrificed before the sage can recognize the hieroglyphic as hieroglyphic. La Fontaine arrives just at the moment in the history of Western culture when the sage's work has already been done. The world has already been read; hieroglyphics have already been written. La Fontaine does not find, as did his sage, a world of events to read and write as hieroglyphics, but already textualized fragments that need to be undone, deconstructed. In Chapter 4, I will show this process at work in "Les Deux Pigeons," a fable whose title and opening verses place it clearly within the hieroglyphic tradition.

2
Book, Brain, Body: Citation and the Scene of Reading

"Démocrite et les Abdéritains"

> *Qu'est-ce que le cerveau humain, sinon un palimpseste immense et naturel? Mon cerveau est un palimpseste et le vôtre aussi, lecteur.*
>
> Baudelaire
> "Les Paradis artificiels"

Taken on its most superficial level, "Démocrite et les Abdéritains" (*Fables* 8.26) almost seems to be playing at the parlor game known as Contrary Proverbs. One player cites an old saw, a proverb, or a well-known quotation; the opponent counters with another saying that conveys the opposite meaning. Points are given for cleverness: "Thou shalt not steal" answers "God helps those who help themselves." In a somewhat similar manner, the opening verse of this fable pits a paraphrase of Horace's "Odi profanum vulgus et arceo" (*Odes* 3.1) against the well-worn adage *vox populi, vox dei* in the closing verse of the fable. Along the way, a biblical allusion, an allusion to the Delphic inscription, and a maxim create a backdrop of allusion and citation against which the fable's story itself unfolds. What is the function of these allusions, and, perhaps more importantly, of "allusiveness" or "citationality" in general in this fable? To what extent do these echoes of other voices, these reverberations of other texts, condition the reader's reception of this fable? In this chapter, I will need to examine how the game that this fable seems to be playing with the texts to which it alludes is related to the moral or political significance of the fable. Is it the truth of the adage *vox populi, vox dei* that is put into question here, or does the adage retroactively undo the specifically antidemocratic ideology on which the fable seems to be based? In either case, we will see, the discourse of wisdom figured in these proverbs is turned against itself.

Against this backdrop of allusion and citation, another tale of wisdom and folly unfolds. Despite the narrator's insistence that the Abdéritains are crazy and Démocrite wise, the interrogative note on which the fable closes permits an element of doubt, or at least lets us wonder about the difference, that very fine line that separates, and binds. As in "Le Fou qui vend la sagesse," the fable's diagnosis of folly depends curiously, or perhaps not so curiously, on an astute interrogation of acts of reading. The Abdéritains interpret Démocrite's words and actions as signs of his madness, which they attribute to too much reading. Hippocrate, the legendary founder of medical semiotics, arrives on the scene to find Démocrite absorbed in an extraordinarily ambiguous scene of reading. The narrator himself is obliged to close his fable with a question mark, since the story he has just told gives the lie to the adage he claims to have read in a "certain place." I will be obliged to see how the representation and interpretation of acts of reading in the story are related to the allusive, citational mode in which much of the fable is written and how the problematics of reading and speaking, of voice and text, find their place within the opposition of madness and common sense.

The fable of "Démocrite et les Abdéritains" takes place in four movements. A narrator speaking in the first person opens and closes the fable, bracketing the story of Démocrite within his own discourse. As the fable opens, the narrator rails against the people and their faulty judgment, states the central premise of the fable (namely, that the people are unqualified judges), and cites the case of Démocrite in support of this thesis. In the story proper, the people of Abdera send a deputation to Hippocrate asking for his help in restoring Démocrite to sanity. Hippocrate arrives to find Démocrite absorbed in his work. Although neither Démocrite's nor Hippocrate's words are reported in the fable, the reader is to conclude, the narrator tells us in the final moment, that this story proves the original thesis that the people are a "juge récusable." Finally, the adage *vox populi, vox dei* is literally put into (a) question.

***

Que j'ai toujours haï les pensers du vulgaire!
Qu'il me semble profane, injuste, et téméraire;

Book, Brain, Body 23

> Mettant de faux milieux entre la chose et lui,
> Et mesurant par soi ce qu'il voit en autrui!
> Le maître d'Epicure en fit l'apprentissage.
> Son pays le crut fou: Petits esprits! mais quoi?
>   Aucun n'est prophète chez soi.
> Ces gens étaient les fous, Démocrite le sage.

"Démocrite et les Abdéritains" thus opens with a not so subtle paraphrase of one of the best-known verses of Roman antiquity. The fact of its quotation immediately evokes the Barthesian question "Who is speaking here?" Commentators are surely not wrong in assimilating this narratorial *je* to the Epicurean La Fontaine, even when this narrator clearly is borrowing the words of another. In any case, the fable takes its stand against "les pensers du vulgaire," common knowledge, too common sense, or what Roland Barthes has called *doxa*: "The Doxa . . . is Public Opinion, the mind of the majority, petit bourgeois consensus, the Voice of Nature, the Voice of Prejudice" (*Roland Barthes* 47). Christopher Prendergast has refined Barthes's definition to include "that vast network of utterances, texts, discourses which collectively constitute the space of what the phenomenologists call the 'natural attitude of society'" (262).[1] Considered in these terms, the fable attempts to be *para-doxal* by inscribing its superior wisdom in opposition to *doxa*, what everyone knows to be true.[2] This "opposition," however, is not the simple binary opposition it may seem, but a logical quagmire: "the doxa is a generic concept that includes both itself and paradox as the sub-classes of which it is the overarching class" (Prendergast 276). The fable displays the instability of the system on which it bases its assertions when it musters support for the rightness of its position by citing a proverb. It thus manages to retain the doxal and the para-doxal within its problematic.[3]

In this chapter, I will not be concerned with defining proverbs, allusions, quotations, maxims, sentences, aphorisms, or adages by their shared or distinguishing stylistic features. A vast body of critical literature has taken this task well in hand. I will be primarily interested in what happens when a text adopts, adapts, and displays these other texts and in so doing saturates "citationality" as signified. One operational distinction is, however, in order. Generally speaking, proverbs are distinguished from other modes of citation by their anonymity. They are property that belongs to everyone and no one. Geoffrey Bennington makes this distinction with characteristic precision: "The fact that the proverb is a repetition of a given sequence of signifiers also defines it as a *quotation*, but it is characteristic of the proverb that it is impossible to assign a first utterance of it by appending to the sequence an author's signature: the proverb is in this sense always an anonymous utterance" (*Sententiousness* 16). In every case in this fable, it is likely that seventeenth-century readers would readily append an author's signature to those types of citation I have been calling proverbs. The significant exception is the concluding paraphrase of *vox populi, vox dei,* to which the fable itself ascribes a first use, an author.

The narrator's adoption and adaptation of Horace's *odi profanum vulgus* serves for most readers to situate the fable within a framework of shared values, most easily identified with Epicureanism. What happens when a citation in effect loses its signature in order to become a proverb, as in the case of the biblical phrase become the proverbial "Aucun n'est prophète chez soi"? It is intriguing to restore the signature, to consider this "proverb" as a citation for the purpose of comparing the textual strategies employed by the fable and the biblical text, its source. In fact, Jesus and the fable employ similar rhetorical strategies. Jesus substitutes his own declaration, "Nemo propheta acceptus est in patria sua" (Luke 4.24), preceded by the Hebraism "Amen . . ." used in the Gospels only by Jesus for his most solemn declarations (R. Brown, *Jerome Biblical Commentary* 2: 131), for a proverb: "dicetis mihi hanc similitudinem medice cura te ipsum" ("You will quote me this proverb, 'Physician cure yourself' ") (Luke 4.23).[4]

***

L'erreur alla si loin qu'Abdère députa
    Vers Hippocrate, et l'invita,
    Par lettres et par ambassade,
A venir rétablir la raison du malade.
Notre concitoyen, disaient-ils en pleurant,
Perd l'esprit: la lecture a gâté Démocrite.
Nous l'estimerions plus s'il était ignorant.
Aucun nombre, dit-il, les mondes ne limite:
    Peut-être même ils sont remplis
    De Démocrites infinis.
Non content de ce songe il y joint des atomes,
Enfants d'un cerveau creux, invisibles fantômes;
Et, mesurant les cieux sans bouger d'ici-bas,
Il connaît l'univers et ne se connaît pas.

Book, Brain, Body 25

The Abdéritains' embassy to Hippocrate is marked by a curious attitude toward Démocrite and his erudition. Démocrite has lost his mind because of too much reading. This is the first incidence of the theme of reading that I will watch grow in importance as the fable unfolds. Reading is the cause of Démocrite's madness; his aberrant scientific theories are its symptoms. As proof, the ambassadors, speaking in one voice ("disaient-ils"), cite Démocrite's more extravagant claims: infinite worlds, atoms, measuring the skies. The report of these fantasies prepares the generalizing statement, which, for the Abdéritains, summarizes Démocrite's case: "Il connaît l'univers et ne se connaît pas."

The people, it seems, are capable of irony. If Démocrite's theories are merely signs of his folly, the first part of the statement intensifies the negation in the second part. Démocrite does not "know" the universe, and he knows himself even less. However, the people's statement is rhetorically more complex than an ironic reading reveals. The reader ought to see in this verse an allusion to the Delphic inscription "Know thyself." The people's statement cites this inscription, and thus pays homage to the conventional wisdom it represents while reducing it to *doxa*, what everyone knows. The people's authority, so to speak, derives in part from their ability to cite this text. At this late stage in Western civilization, after Plato, after Montaigne, after Renaissance humanism, the Delphic injunction, even in the people's deformed version of it, now connotes, paradoxically, the great undefined body of doxal "wisdom." However, the logic and grammar of the original has been transformed from a general injunction to a constative statement about Démocrite. This deflection is highly strategic in that it leaves no space outside of its own reach. By its structure, its self-conscious use of parallelism, this statement resembles an aphorism. One is tempted to read in this statement the application in the people's discourse of a maxim about humans in general to the particular, exemplary case of Démocrite. The people's statement ("*Il* connaît l'univers [. . .]") presupposes a generalized maxim: "*On* connaît l'univers [. . .]." This (fictive) maxim, from which the people's reading derives, contains a good part of the Enlightenment critique of the limits of philosophy. It might, for example, serve as hypogram for Voltaire's *Micromégas*, whose final chapter turns on various philosophers' responses to Micromégas's observation: "Puisque vous savez si bien ce qui est hors de vous, sans doute vous savez encore mieux ce qui est en dedans"(119).

At the very end of their petition, the people reveal that their interest in Démocrite's case is not entirely disinterested:

> Un temps fut qu'il savait accorder les débats;
> Maintenant il parle à lui-même.

The people want their Démocrite back. The sane Démocrite was useful; crazy Démocrite talks to himself. Démocrite's speech once was capable of resolving differences; it is now directed nowhere, or rather inward. For the Abdéritains, Démocrite's talking to himself is the ultimate sign of his alienation in that it represents a perversion of what he once was. The people in their invitation to Hippocrate clearly valorize useful speech ("accorder les débats") at the expense of Démocrite's empty ("cerveau creux") and self-centered ("il parle à lui-même") erudition. Books are the problem; too much reading leads to madness. Even the redundancy in the communication of their request to Hippocrate underlines their primordial "logocentrism," and their naive distrust of the written. As if letters alone were not sufficient to communicate their message, they invite the physician "par lettres *et* par ambassade." This minor detail proleptically exhibits an understated thematic opposition between voice and text, an opposition on which the people rely to build their case for Démocrite's madness. This theme, which I have already broached in another guise in the previous chapter on "Le Fou qui vend la sagesse," will be one of our principal considerations in Chapter 5, devoted to *Psyché*.

***

What do the people want from Démocrite? In a word, they want him to live up to his name, to exercise the moral imperative inscribed therein. They are in a sense asking Doctor Hippocrate to restore Démocrite to his name. In form, both *Démocrite* and *Hippocrate* resemble those literary Greek-based stage names that in the seventeenth century revealed the essence of a character. If Greek-sounding names could be forged to reveal the essence of a "character," could not names that already exist be put to use as textual generators in their own right? As it happens, *Démocrite* is easily read as a name composed of *demos* ("the people," *le vulgaire*) + *crites* ("judge"). There is even evidence to suggest that the name *Démocrite* was read as antonomasia for "critic" throughout the Renaissance and seventeenth century (Beugnot, "Démocrite" 539; Jehasse). In seventeenth-century France, literary names were forged from Greek stems, but their syntax was often ambiguous. Should the protagonist's name be read as "judge of the people" or "judged by the

Book, Brain, Body

people," as the word *demo-cracy* means "rule by the people"? La Fontaine's fable activates both possibilities, thereby refusing to solve the syntactic dilemma. The people accuse Démocrite of being a failed judge ("Un temps fut qu'il savait accorder les débats"); the narrator will level the same accusation against the people themselves: "Le peuple est juge récusable."

Hippocrate's name, like his role in the story, is more problematic. While no leader of horses (*Hippocrate = hippos + crates,* "leader") is called for, *hippos* may serve as a metonym for the animal world evoked in this fable by the explicit opposition of animal to human. ("[Démocrite] Cherchait dans l'homme *et* dans la bête / Quel siège a la raison [. . .].") Démocrite's scientific research, we will see, serves to reduce the difference between the animal and the human. Perhaps the people want more from the contact of Démocrite and Hippocrate than a cure, restoration of Démocrite's name. The plot of this fable can be seen as a sort of chiasmatic game with the names of the two named characters. The people want a *Demo-crate*; they get a *Hippo-crites.*

***

Hippocrate arrives at the people's bidding to find Démocrite, who, according to his fellow countrymen, had lost his senses while looking for the site of reason, that is, its physical location in the body:

> [. . .] Hippocrate arriva dans le temps
> Que celui qu'on disait n'avoir raison ni sens
> Cherchait dans l'homme et dans la bête
> Quel siège a la raison, soit le cœur, soit la tête.

The paradox of "Démocrite" is similar to that of "Le Fou qui vend la sagesse." How can one who has lost his mind locate its site? Yet contrary to "Le Fou qui vend la sagesse," the ostensible strategy of this fable is to deny the original diagnosis, the people's, in favor of expert opinion, Hippocrate's. The texture of the sentence that states this paradox is as interesting as the paradox itself. The sentence is built on a triple series of details, each of which turns on a coordinating conjunction: "n'avoir raison *ni* sens"; "dans l'homme *et* dans la bête"; "*soit* le cœur, *soit* la tête." Of course, each of these incidences of coordination is explicable in terms of the poet's philosophical opinions.[5] The head and the heart were in Greek science two contenders for the honor of housing the faculty of reason. La Fontaine does not mention that the "historical" Democritus placed the seat of our intellectual activity in the heart (Régnier 2: 344 n20). In La Fontaine's source for this fable, Hippocrates's apocryphal letters, Democritus is not searching for the seat of reason, but the origin of *atra bilis*, black bile, the humor responsible for melancholy. Readers familiar with La Fontaine's source could appreciate his clever substitution of reason for black bile.[6] However, looking for the seat of reason in animals as well as in man was not for La Fontaine one more sign of folly, but proof of Démocrite's good sense and, more than incidentally, a barb tossed at Descartes. La Fontaine's *parti pris des animaux* is vested in his philosophical convictions as well as in his vocation as literary fabulist. His "Discours à Madame de la Sablière," published with Book 9 of the *Fables* (1679), takes up just this problem of thought in animals. In the "Discours," La Fontaine pretends at first to agree with Descartes that animals are unthinking machines:

> Or vous savez, Iris, de certaine science,
> Que, quand la bête penserait,
> La bête ne réfléchirait
> Sur l'objet ni sur sa pensée.
> Descartes va plus loin, et soutient nettement
> Qu'elle ne pense nullement.
> Vous n'êtes point embarrassée
> De le croire, ni moi. Cependant, [. . .]

What follows this "cependant" subverts Descartes's theory by dint of examples of animals that do indeed appear to think. Démocrite's research into the seat of reason in man and in animals thus anticipates La Fontaine's own conclusions.

Readers, of course, approach the text from another direction entirely. One should not overlook the obvious textural pattern created by three incidences of coordinate phrasing merely because each incidence is pertinent to an extratextual philosophical argument. The repetition of this stylistic device within a single sentence, one incidence per verse, produces a symmetrical structure that is in itself striking. For Jean Dominique Biard, symmetry in the sentence structure gives "une structure symétrique à tout un passage, et par suite, ordre et clarté à toute la fable" (209). It is almost as if the simple binary oppositions within the narrator's depiction of Démocrite reveal the order and clarity of Démocrite's mind that is questioned by the Abdéritains but confirmed by

Hippocrate. This striking binary patterning in this passage will, however, give way in the next few verses to a different spatial and textual model, that of the labyrinth. In other words, the symmetrical structure discovered by Biard, rather than ordering the whole fable in its own image or serving as a metaphor for the mind of Démocrite, here exists only to be undone, to be displaced by another metaphor and to stand in opposition to it.[7]

At this point readers might begin to suspect that this rigidly symmetrical structure is modeled on another text from which it draws its syntactic strength.[8] One might even remember that these same oppositions are operative in Descartes's *Discours de la méthode*. The second paragraph of the "Première Partie" in fact actualizes the first two: "[. . .] pour *la raison, ou le sens*, d'autant qu'elle est la seule chose *qui nous rend hommes et nous distingue des bêtes*, je veux croire qu'elle est toute entière en un chacun" (1: 568-69; my emphasis). It is worth recalling at this point that Descartes's famous "bon sens" is what Démocrite has been accused by the people, that other repository of "bon sens," of having lost. The "Cinquième Partie" is concerned precisely with the difference between humans and animals. Descartes attributes this difference to "cette partie distincte du corps dont il a été dit ci-dessus que la nature n'est que de penser," without which "les animaux sans raison nous ressemblent" (1: 619). What follows this influential analysis of difference and similarity with respect to animals and humans has considerable interest for La Fontaine's fable:

> Mais afin qu'on puisse voir en quelle sorte j'y traitais cette matière, je veux mettre ici 'explication du mouvement du cœur et des artères, qui, étant le premier et le plus général qu'on observe dans les animaux, on jugera facilement de lui ce qu'on doit penser de tous les autres. Et afin qu'on ait moins de difficulté à entendre ce que j'en dirai, je voudrais que ceux qui ne sont point versés dans l'anatomie prissent la peine, avant que de lire ceci, de faire couper devant eux le cœur de quelque grand animal [. . .]. (1: 619-20)

Readers are explicitly invited to put down their books ("avant que de lire ceci") and to dissect the heart of some large animal. What kind of authorial strategy is at work here? In any case, both La Fontaine's fable and Descartes's *Discours* display a similar pattern of oppositions between *raison* and [*bon*] *sens*, humans and animals, the heart and the head. These oppositions are modeled in the *Discours* and then stylistically heightened in the fable by a series of coordinations.

Each incidence of coordination in the fable marks a choice of possible actualizations, a route through an intertextual labyrinth. The *Discours* chooses to develop *raison*, humans, and the heart; the fable will treat "good sense" (*doxa*), humans and animals (that is, as a single set rather than as opposing terms), and, as we will see, the brain. I have already studied another incidence of the same strategy, the same manner of relating the fable to another text. The Abdéritains' invitation to Hippocrate was communicated "par lettres *et* par ambassade." La Fontaine's source for this fable was these apocryphal letters.[9] The fable chooses to actualize the Abdéritains' deputation for the reasons I have demonstrated. What is significant at this point is that the fable in every instance encodes its relation to its intertext by a syntactic coordination.

Once the reader has placed the Cartesian intertext, Démocrite's story may be read as the inversion of Descartes's. Even their names suggest each other, sharing five of six phonemes. This inversion is particularly striking in the following passage in which Démocrite is placed within a scene, a *locus amoenus*, whose decor may now be seen as a semiotic inversion of Descartes's *poêle*; "exteriority" substitutes for "interiority" as "nature" for "culture."

> Sous un ombrage épais, assis près d'un ruisseau,
>   Les labyrinthes d'un cerveau
> L'occupaient. Il avait à ses pieds maint volume,
> Et ne vit presque pas son ami s'avancer,
>   Attaché selon sa coutume.

While the seventeenth-century language tolerated somewhat more easily than the modern language the adjectival modifiers in the first verse referring to the direct object pronoun rather than to the grammatical subject of the sentence, and while a strong *rejet* followed by a syntactic break and hiatus ("L'occupaient. // Il [. . .]") may well have been allowed in minor poetic genres, the grammatical and rhythmic texture of these verses contrasts sharply with the overwhelming effect of symmetry observed in the preceding verses. On another level, placing Démocrite within a landscape provides an internal transition by shifting readers' attention from a theoretical statement of Démocrite's research project to a concrete scene—research in progress. It is clear at least that the reader is invited to consider here a representation of a body doing something within a decor. The significance of the passage, and of the fable, depends in part on readers' naturalization of this central scene.[10]

Apart from the mere fact reported almost in passing that Hippocrate

Book, Brain, Body

discussed ("ayant [. . .] raisonné") philosophical matters with Démocrite, a supposed *fou,* readers' opinions of Démocrite may be informed only through this scene, unmediated by "faux milieux entre la chose et lui." For the purposes of the fable's argument, the narrator's own discourse must be deemed transparent, a "true" *milieu.* What then is Démocrite supposed to be doing? Our answer will turn on our reading of "Les labyrinthes d'un cerveau," clearly figurative language, which in the seventeenth century, was not supposed to be problematic: "The figure is an ornament which does not trouble the representational function of language" (Culler, *Poetics* 135). To make a scene of these verses, the reader will need to bring them into a discursive order that seems natural within the categories allowed by seventeenth-century discourse. Such an activity is essentially intertextual in that the coherence readers attempt to reclaim for this scene is a function of its relation to other texts.

In a laconic note on "Les labyrinthes d'un cerveau," Georges Couton (ed. Couton, *Fables* 497) asks whether this extraordinary phrase is not original with La Fontaine: "Sens figuré créé par La Fontaine?" Perhaps it was, but what is neither original, nor unique, nor less interesting for that fact, is the figure of the labyrinth. This figure is perhaps particularly striking to the modern reader, since it recurs in contemporary avant-garde literature with a frequency and force that borders on the obsessional. In an essay on "Cybernetics and Ghosts," Italo Calvino recounts the main lines of an essay by Hans Magnus Enzensberger in which the German poet and critic wonders about the meaning of literature's fascination with this figure as it appears from ancient times to the very recent work of Borges and Robbe-Grillet. One must admit that La Fontaine's contemporaries were no less fascinated by labyrinthine structures than readers of Robbe-Grillet, Borges, Eco, or Calvino, as Racine's *Phèdre* or *Bajazet* will suffice to show. La Fontaine, too, perhaps deserves a modest place in the history of one of modernity's most persistent metaphors. Richard Danner has proposed the labyrinth as a structural metaphor and as heuristic device for reading Book 10 of the *Fables,* although the word does not itself occur in Book 10.[11] What is interesting to note at this point is that modern scientific discourse and one of modernity's most compelling textual figures seem to emerge concurrently in late seventeenth-century France and that they are juxtaposed in this particular fable.

The fortunes of the figure of the labyrinth from La Fontaine's day to our own add interest retrospectively to this extraordinary figure as it is used in the fable. Analysis of the figure will allow us to propose at the outset three possible answers to the simple question about what Démocrite is represented as doing: (1) Démocrite is meditating, (2) Démocrite is dissecting, or (3) Démocrite is reading.

Démocrite is meditating, that is, Démocrite is somehow attempting to locate the seat of reason within himself. This naturalization relies on a figurative reading of *cerveau*. While the term in the seventeenth century primarily designated "la substance moëlleuse & blanche, froide et humide enfermée dans la tête de l'homme" (Furetière, *cerveau*), the language did authorize figurative uses as in the locution *cerveau creux* (cited by Furetière).[12] In this fable, the people in their complaint against Démocrite term his atoms "Enfants d'un cerveau creux." The figurative use of the word in the "false" discourse of the people invites a figurative reading when the word is seen again in the "truthful" discourse of the narrator. "Les labyrinthes d'un cerveau" corrects the people's mistaken opinion by substituting the labyrinth for "emptiness" as the architectural metaphor for Démocrite's brain. Perhaps there is a bit here too of what John Lapp has felicitously called "sunken images."[13] Démocrite's meditation, his descent into the labyrinths of his own brain, makes of Démocrite a new Theseus, as if the thinking center of his being, a Cartesian *res cogitans*, could be tracked to its lair like the Minotaur. This sunken mythological image leaves perhaps its trace in the word *attaché*, whose literal meaning might recall Ariadne's thread.

Démocrite is dissecting. Perhaps Démocrite is to be imagined as the prototypical anatomist rather than as the Cartesian meditator, or as Descartes the anatomist rather than as the Descartes of the *Discours* or the *Méditations*. The lines of perception I am tracing within this tableau turn from radical interiority, introspection, speculation, to the exteriorized, observable, objectified brain.[14] Of course, the skull as emblem of death and scenes of meditation on a skull (for example, Georges de La Tour's *Madeleine* or Shakespeare's Hamlet and Yorick) are baroque commonplaces. The brain, however, is something else again. In this case, readers take "les labyrinthes d'un cerveau" for a visual metaphor for the outward convoluted appearance of the brain. As Georges Couton has pointed out, Furetière does not mention this metaphoric use of *labyrinthe* in the article *labyrinthe*; it does however occur in the article *cerveau*. This article is relatively long for Furetière (almost one and a half columns) and is noteworthy for its anatomic detail as well as for its dutiful citation of authors both ancient and modern. Here is the section relevant to our concerns:

> Ils [les antérieurs et supérieurs ventricules] ont plusieurs plis et replis, & font plusieurs tours & retours qu'on appelle *choroïdes,* par le moyen

d'un tissu ou lacis de petites veines & artères en forme de labyrinthe qu'on appelle *rets admirable*.

Labyrinthe refers here, of course, to a part of the brain and not to its overall physical appearance. I cite this passage as an example of early scientific rhetoric whose metaphoric system ("plis et replis"; "tours et retours") in this passage might very well rely on "labyrinth" as textual generator.

This naturalization, in many ways the most disturbing, the most scandalous of the three I have proposed, is the only one it can be certain La Fontaine knew about. In La Fontaine's source, the series of apocryphal letters exchanged by Democritus and Hippocrates, Hippocrates arrives to find Democritus surrounded by books and by dissected animals:

> Sur ses genoux, Démocrite avait très soigneusement posé un livre; quelques autres jonchaient le sol de par et d'autre, près d'un amoncellement d'animaux entièrement disséqués. (*Sur le rire et la folie* 74)

In La Fontaine's text, the dissected animals seem to have been replaced entirely by books: "Il avait à ses pieds maint volume." One can conclude from this evidence that La Fontaine more or less consciously attenuated the possibility for naturalizing this scene as a dissection without eliminating it altogether. This is perhaps the propitious moment to recall Descartes's recommendation to his reader (cited above) to dissect the heart of an animal before reading further. In this naturalizing fiction, Démocrite complies, but chooses the head rather than the heart.

The explicit mention of books within this scene and the curious juxtaposition of reading to dissection in the Cartesian intertext brings us to the third prospect: *Démocrite is reading*. The paratactic series of sentences without coordinating conjunctions would seem to indicate a causal link between the volumes at Démocrite's feet and his absorption in whatever it is he is doing. On another level, the etymology of *volume* (from *volumen* < *volvere*, "to roll, to twist around") repeats the topological structure of the labyrinth.

One constant emerges from the overlay of naturalizing fictions I have tried to describe. Démocrite is figured as a reader whose text is variously his mind, a brain (of an animal, no doubt), or a book. No matter how readers of the fable represent what is "happening" in this scene, the text resolutely displays the curious interpenetration of textual and corporeal figures. The scene is not reducible to a single fiction that will allow its complete naturalization, its recuperation as a representation of an action in the world. While naturalization as a readerly strategy for making sense is both necessary and doomed to failure, I am interested here in the palimpsest of superimposed readings invited by the text, in the essential intertextuality of the reading process as figured in this scene of reading. Within this scene, readers perceive a series of anomalies that cannot be simply explained away by inserting them in a naturalizing fiction. However, a single literary piece, if the *Discours de la méthode* can be called that, provides a model with which this fable is systematically at variance. I should stress at this point that the residue, the remains, of these superimposed readings is not a subject; it is not "Démocrite." The subject/object dichotomy I have maintained in my account of plausible naturalizations of this passage is even subverted by the grammar of the sentence: "Démocrite" is the grammatical object of the verb rather than its subject: "Les labyrinthes d'un cerveau / L'occupaient."

In his recent essay entitled *The Tremulous Private Body*, Francis Barker recounts the emergence of modern corporeality, "what was done to us in the seventeenth century" (68), through texts by Pepys, Descartes, Marvell, and a painting by Rembrandt, "each organized, knowingly or not, around the body, its dangers and its uses" (103). The modern body, according to Barker, is "pressed back across representation and then rehabilitated within the model and the distribution of a mode of discourse that will only readmit the body at the price of its figuration in not, at last, speech, but text" (104). This process seems to be at work as well in La Fontaine's fable. As Barker reads it, Rembrandt's *The Anatomy Lesson of Dr. Nicolaas Tulp* offers a visual confirmation of the kind of scene that I see at work through the fable's textual palimpsest.[15] At the center of the painting lies the cadaver, the body of a criminal. Dr. Tulp points out for the viewers (the viewers of the painting, that is; or the fictive audience at the public dissection Rembrandt's painting commemorates) the "grossly over-large" an "anatomically inaccurate" hand of the thief (Barker 79).[16] It is, of course, right and just that the thief's hand suffer this postmortem indignity, just as, perhaps, the philosopher's brain should be the object of particular scrutiny. Yet no line of sight within this painting touches the body of the criminal.The attending surgeons' gazes pass over the dissected hand; to a man, they fix their stare at the volume open at the cadaver's feet. What Démocrite's scene of reading renders ambiguous, Rembrandt's makes explicit, almost as if Rembrandt's cast of characters were conflated in Démocrite's scene. As Barker concludes, "[t]his modern division-and-rule of the corporal operates across the painting and across its subsequent dispersion a dual strategy in respect of the body: of exclusion—of blindness—and of

Book, Brain, Body

textualization" (Barker 80; his emphasis). I would claim that "Démocrite et les Abdéritains" operates a similar strategy with respect to the body and the text.

***

> Leur compliment fut court, ainsi qu'on peut penser.
> Le sage est ménager du temps et des paroles.
> Ayant donc mis à part les entretiens frivoles,
> Et beaucoup raisonné sur l'homme et sur l'esprit,
> Ils tombèrent sur la morale.

Contrary to our expectations, Hippocrate's arrival on the scene does not serve to frame a philosophical dialogue. We learn nothing about what Démocrite and Hippocrate said to each other, since their speech is reported neither in direct nor in indirect discourse. Three verses, however, convey their lack of interest in small talk, while two merely list the subjects broached. Readers might even be taken aback by a certain disproportion between the ostensible purpose of their meeting—to determine the state of Démocrite's mind and, incidentally, to communicate a "philosophical" message—and the literary realization of this scene. The fable seems more interested in denigrating idle chatter than in reporting serious discourse. After the essentially unnaturalizable scene of reading I have just examined, the scene of dialogue, the point toward which the whole fable has been directed, is disappointing in its brevity. The fable does, however, do its utmost to reveal its strategy for rendering this scene conventional in every respect. It is right and natural for philosophers to have little time to waste on social graces "ainsi qu'on peut penser." This doxal wisdom is even condensed into a maxim: "Le sage est ménager du temps et des paroles," whose form alone is sufficient to guarantee the *vraisemblance* of the scene (Genette, *Figures II* 71-99).

A maxim at this point in the fable is of some interest, since the fable as a whole, as we have seen, is built on a number of textual fragments inserted strategically into the fable by an anthologizing narrator. It is thus in some respects not surprising to find the poet trying his hand, so to speak, at writing his own maxim. Régnier attests to the success of the maxim: "Vers devenu proverbe" (2: 345). The fable that thematizes and problematizes the collection and display of previously textualized fragments contributes its own effort to the doxal anthology. Of course, this is not a feature unique to this fable.

La Fontaine's fables and tales are veritable *machines à citation*, quotability being one sign of literarity in the seventeenth century.

The very brief recapitulation of Démocrite's and Hippocrate's excluded dialogue tells us nothing whatever about the philosophers' opinions, other than that they were discussed. The reader must conclude that for the purposes of the fable, the content of the message is less important than the fact of its communication. Things happen somewhat differently when "Ils tombèrent sur la morale." The word *morale* functions here on two levels. Within the *récit*, *morale* is a branch of philosophy, the object of the philosophers' discussion; in the narration, *morale* is taken to mean a structural part of the fable. This usage is well attested in the *Fables*, especially in the critical prologue to Book 6:

> Une Morale nue apporte de l'ennui;
> Le conte fait passer le précepte avec lui.
>
> (*Fables* 6.1)

Here *morale* and *conte* are used in approximately the same relation as *moralité* and *fable* in the structural definition of the apologue on whose metaphoric system I will have more to say in the next chapter: "L'Apologue est composé de deux parties, dont on peut appeler l'une le Corps, l'autre l'Ame. Le Corps est la Fable; l'Ame, la Moralité" (*Fables*, Préface 10). The word *morale* can thus function to shift between narrative and narration. If the *morale* represents the finality of the fable, its purpose and *raison d'être*, it also represents its end, as if mention of *morale* has closural force in the fable.[17]

The parallel movement of the *récit* and its telling reveals a thematic disproportion I have noted in another context. The denigration of idle speech on one level seems to motivate the elision of serious discourse on another. The narratorial *je* then returns to comment on the fable's telling of the story, to justify the exclusion of the expected dialogue and proclaim the sufficiency of the *récit* to the conclusion both of the story and of the fable as a whole:

> Il n'est pas besoin que j'étale
> Tout ce que l'un et l'autre dit.
> Le récit précédent suffit
> Pour montrer que le peuple est juge récusable.

According to the narrator, this story is sufficient to prove the people wrong about Démocrite. It is finally Hippocrate's prestige, his name, his *renom*, that

Book, Brain, Body

now authenticates the narrator's judgment, stated early in the fable, that "Ces gens étaient les fous, Démocrite le sage." The self-sufficient *récit* is in this fable rather a meeting of names than of minds. The narrator's explicit refusal to narrate the scene of dialogue contrasts sharply with the people's detailed exposition of their case against Démocrite.

The maxim "Le peuple est juge récusable," which encapsulates the lesson purportedly demonstrated by this fable, contradicts one of our most durable adages, *vox populi, vox dei:*

> En quel sens est donc véritable
> Ce que j'ai lu dans certain lieu,
> Que sa voix est la voix de Dieu?

The fable, whose narratorial "voice," we have seen, is a collage of unattributed quotations, now specifically cites a textual source for the adage put into question by the story of Démocrite and Hippocrate: "ce que j'ai lu dans certain lieu." Readers of this fable readily take "certain lieu" (modern syntax would prefer "*un* certain lieu") for the Bible, a text whose proverbs may not be so easily contradicted by a lowly fable. Chamfort, for example, sees it this way: "La Fontaine prend l'air du doute, par respect pour l'Ecriture, dont ces paroles sont tirées" (Chamfort 142; qtd. in Régnier 2: 345). The clash of contradictory proverbs, we might think, is to be solved by authority, as was the case of Démocrite's sanity. As we have seen, the fable judged Démocrite sane on Hippocrate's authority alone, withholding whatever it would take for readers to form their own conclusions. But which "authority" will now prevail, the voice of the narrator, or the voice of the people recognized as the voice of God by the Scriptures themselves? If, for the implied reader of the fable, the statement "the voice of the people [is] the voice of God" is true by the authority of the Scriptures, then one's task ought to be to answer literally the fable's question "In what sense ...?" Readers ought to seek strategies to show that apparent conflict between the sense of the fable and the sense of the adage is illusory. Is this a rhetorical question or not? The problem is further enriched by the fact that despite the narrator's insistence that he read the proverb "dans certain lieu," the proverb is not to be found in the Bible. This false attribution of a well-known proverb would very likely not be noticed, since in the unlikely case the reader had reason to doubt the narrator's word, few readers are so scrupulous as to read the entire Bible to prove empirically that the proverb is not there, somewhere. Chamfort's reading is probably typical of most readers.[18]

What I find fascinating in all of this is that of all the texts this fable cites, the only one the narrator specifically marks as citation is also the only one that in fact has no objectively verifiable "first" use, no "source" at all in the modern, positivist sense. Why is the narrator (or La Fontaine) mistaken (or lying)?

If La Fontaine, Chamfort, and even Pope Sylvester II were mistaken about the textual source of this adage, modern scholarship has shown that they were not far wrong in situating it within the Judeo-Christian tradition (Boas 1; Gallacher) and even within what might be termed a biblical intertext. The Bible indeed does use similar phrasing, for example, in the Vulgate translation of 1 Samuel 8. In this chapter, the people ask God for a king; Samuel demurs, but God commands him to listen to the voice of the people: "dixit autem Dominus ad Samuhel audi vocem populi in omnibus quae loquuntur tibi nonenim te abiecerunt sed me ne regnem super eos." ("The Lord said to Samuel: Listen to the voice of the people in everything they say to you, for they have not rejected you, but me, so that I not reign over them.") While it is in fact the voice of God that commands Samuel to listen to the voice of the people, the text does not identify the two voices. The point of the chapter is rather that the people are wrong in asking for a king and that God will answer their request with punishment.[19]

Of course, the fact that *vox populi, vox dei* is assimilated to the biblical intertext does not mean La Fontaine did not in fact read it in any number of places. Boas and Gallacher cite many legal, political, and literary texts from the Carolingian period through the seventeenth century in which this adage is quoted, none of which, however, is of sufficient prestige to rival the Bible as La Fontaine's "certain lieu." A curious tendency does nonetheless emerge from a paradigmatic reading of pre-Enlightenment citations of this adage. In the vast majority of cases, the adage is cited disapprovingly, or ironically, or is contradicted or revised. Given the political situation of the times, it is not surprising that few would agree with the adage, but it is amazing that it is quoted at all. Troublingly paradoxical adages, it would seem, are best forgotten. Yet from its earliest history (and prehistory in the Samuel episode), this adage seems to exist in order to be contradicted. I suspect that the adage owes its survival as textual fragment to its various refutations. One example from La Fontaine's century will suffice to demonstrate the tendency to revision that this proverb seems to inspire.[20] Pierre Corneille revises the proverb in Camille's monarchist profession of faith:

> Ces mêmes dieux à Tulle ont inspiré ce choix;
> Et la voix du public n'est pas toujours leur voix;

> Ils descendent bien moins dans de si bas étages
> Que dans l'âme des rois, leurs vivantes images.
> *(Horace* 3.3.841-44)

Corneille's hedging ("pas toujours"), his refusal to contradict absolutely the proverb, may perhaps be a stylistic variation of La Fontaine's discreet rewriting of the proverb as a question. In any event, I must take account of the extraordinary case of a proverb conventionally accorded high prestige, often considered biblical in origin, which almost invariably generates discourse that negates the sense of the proverb. In other words, the para-doxal discourse that aims to refute the very proverb that sacralizes doxal wisdom (*vox populi*) in effect preserves what it seeks to negate by quoting it. La Fontaine's literal putting into question must then be seen, despite and in face of the text's explicit but incorrect statement to the contrary, not as the quotation of an authoritative text, but rather as citation from the (para-doxal) intertextual accretions that have parasitically attached themselves to the proverb.[21]

***

If "Démocrite et les Abdéritains" is best known by most of La Fontaine's readers primarily as a philosophical statement, it also exhibits features that make it a powerful demonstration of seventeenth-century textuality. The central episode in the fable involves a referentially ambiguous but intertextually coherent scene of reading in a fable that opposes reading to speaking, as madness is opposed to common sense. At the same time, the fable, both in its narratorial voice and in the voice of the people, transcribes textual fragments of all kinds—proverbs, maxims, adages, and allusions—while a pattern of intertextuality by antithesis is established with respect to specific texts by Descartes. This fable also opens our way to a consideration of the relation of the body to writing, one of our main considerations in the next chapter.

3
Bodies and Souls: The Intertextual Corpus
"La Laitière et le Pot au lait" and "Le Curé et le Mort"

Jean-Pierre Collinet first drew critical attention to the curious phenomenon of "double fables":

> Certaines fables présentent pour notre propos un intérêt exceptionnel: ce sont celles qui, traitées sous deux formes différentes, apparaissent comme jumelées. [...] Agissant un peu comme un verre grossissant, cette dualité rend plus facilement perceptible, par le jeu des parallélismes ou des oppositions, le délicat travail de la création poétique. (*Le Monde littéraire* 163)

In this chapter, I would like to take up within a double fable, by Collinet's definition, another sort of doubleness, that on which the fable as a genre is founded. In the preface to the first *recueil* (*Fables*, 1668), La Fontaine defines structurally the double nature of the genre he is at work inventing: "L'Apologue est composé de deux parties, dont on peut appeler l'une le Corps, l'autre l'Ame. Le Corps est la Fable; l'Ame, la Moralité" (*Fables*, Préface 10). The author goes on to explain certain differences between the rules of the genre followed by the Ancients and those he will be following (in the fictive order of the book, in which prefaces always precede the literary work), or rather has followed (in the actual order of composition of the fables). He stresses that one thing alone is essential, and common to all the fabulists who have preceded him: "[...] la Moralité, dont aucun [fabuliste] ne se dispense." No rule lacks an exception and the author goes on to explain that he has found occasion to dispense with an explicit *moralité,* but "ce n'a été que dans les endroits où elle [la moralité] n'a pu entrer avec grâce, et où il est aisé au lecteur de la suppléer."[1] For three centuries this primary articulation in the fable has sustained intense critical interest, and numerous excellent studies have concentrated on the various functions of story and moral in the fable.[2]

There is, however, another way that this central problem might be approached. In this chapter, I will explore the originary metaphor of body and soul at work in the text as it grounds the discourse on which the genre and the fables under consideration as instances of that genre are built. I will be showing as well how these two fables appeal to and problematize the founding metaphor of the fable genre by thematizing bodies and souls as textual metaphors. The site for this investigation will be two fables, "La Laitière et le Pot au lait" and "Le Curé et le Mort," which are related thematically and intertextually, and happen to be juxtaposed as fables 9 and 10 in Book 7 of the *Fables*. In other words, these fables are double fables by Collinet's standards, and by Georges Couton's, too. Couton compares this double fable to the classic example "Le Héron—La Fille" (*Fables* 7.4), while noting a significant difference. In the case of "La Laitière" and "Le Curé," La Fontaine did not join the two into a single fable as he had with "Le Héron—La Fille." "Souci de bienséance?" Couton asks (473). What is the nature of the protection afforded by separating two fables that could very well have been a single text?

Of course, La Fontaine did not invent the scriptural metaphor of body and soul, but seems to have adapted it from the theory of the emblem. Writing in 1662, Claude-François Ménestrier uses the same metaphor in discussing the structure of the emblem: "Les deux parties de ce beau composé, sont les figures, & leur signification, ou leur sens moral, qui est l'âme de ce corps, et la forme qui leur donne toute leur beauté" (*L'Art des emblèmes* 50; qtd. in Russell 102-03). Ménestrier's description seems to follow the logic inherent in all Western metaphysics. The soul, linked to meaning, "sens moral," the Aristotelean form, and the word, is clearly the dominant partner in this arrangement. The body, the picture of the emblem, is inert and essentially meaningless without the life-giving word.[3]

The question of bodies and souls in Descartes's century was as loaded as it has always been. However, Jacques Derrida's reflections on the role of writing in Western metaphysics can serve to refocus our attention on this primary division in a rather unexpected way. What has always seemed a purely metaphysical question is for Derrida related to the central problem of textuality, the trace, writing, difference:

> [...] l'écriture, la lettre, l'inscription sensible ont toujours été considérées par la tradition occidentale comme le corps et la matière extérieurs à

l'esprit, au souffle, au verbe et au logos. Et le problème de l'âme et du corps est sans doute dérivé du problème de l'écriture auquel il semble—inversement—prêter ses métaphores. (*De la grammatologie* 52)

This chapter will concern itself, then, with the inscription of that original difference, the marking and blurring of boundaries (interiority and exteriority; self and other; soul and body) within writing and, specifically, within the writing of the fable.

***

Of La Fontaine's some two hundred forty fables, only a handful have been shown to lack a textual source for the body of the fable. "Le Curé et le Mort" is one of these.[4] This seeming subservience to a tradition of imitation apparently does not obtain for the moral, the authorial commentary, the "soul" of the fable. From fables in which extended "meditations," longish developments on quickly sketched stories ("L'Astrologue qui se laisse tomber dans un puits" and possibly "La Laitière et le Pot au lait" are cases in point), one might conclude too hastily, romantically, that it is the "soul" of the fable that constitutes the space of the poet's freedom, while the body remains tied to another text that it merely, if brilliantly, repeats. These considerations notwithstanding, the obvious question deserves some attention. Why the all but invariable rule that each fable have its "source," and, more pertinently for our concerns in this chapter, why the exception for "Le Curé et le Mort"? Of course, one of the aims of this series of essays is to demonstrate to what extent the fables and tales are grounded in writing, in rewriting, in glossing other texts whose presence within the fable can be veiled but never occluded. It seems to me that the literary history of these two fables is emblematic of the particular set of problems that binds them together.

***

"La Laitière et le Pot au lait" is the last in a long series of versions of an old story; "Le Curé et le Mort," on the other hand, derives from a *fait divers* of the times.[5] For Collinet, these two fables, these "double fables," present "la particularité d'unir une fiction [. . .] à une anecdote réelle inspirée par l'actualité" (*Le Monde littéraire* 212). The first readers of "Le Curé et le Mort" could thus appreciate this aspect of the fable when it first appeared in 1672, six years before its inclusion in the second *recueil* of 1678 where it found its definitive place after "La Laitière et le Pot au lait." In 1672 readers in the know would no doubt take pleasure in recognizing an apparently well-known anecdote and savor La Fontaine's retelling in a way that deliberately obscures reference to the real world. Time passes, and the tenuous link between the fable and the events of 1672 weaken. A century later, Chamfort found the fable little more than a "méchante historiette" (Chamfort 126; Régnier 2: 157). For readers who approach this fable in an edition lacking the necessary footnote (Is there such a thing?), or for "new" critics who choose to interrogate the fable's language and structure apart from its history as text and the history of its successive readings, the "particularité" noted by Collinet does not exist, is not and cannot be operative in the reader's reading. Nothing in this fable, in its story or in its language, can make us believe that this fable is more closely linked to the news of the day than any other tale or fable. As Roseann Runte, writing on La Fontaine's techniques of narration, put it: "La Fontaine assigns equal authority to real and fictional events and characters. In his text *histoire* becomes history" (390). In the case of "Le Curé et le Mort," however, history becomes *histoire*. As I have already noted, La Fontaine usually pays his debts to his literary precursors, while his rare debt to a *fait divers* here goes unpaid.

As for the historical order of the composition of "La Laitière et le Pot au lait" and "Le Curé et le Mort," scholarly opinion is divided. The textual evidence would indicate that "Le Curé et le Mort" was composed first. The editor of the Pléiade edition draws this conclusion from a study of the variants of the 1672 version and the definitive version in the second *recueil*. The first edition alluded in the last verse to the "*farce* du pot au lait" which became the "*fable* du Pot au lait" in the final version. According to this line of reasoning, La Fontaine simply changed the name of the genre after he wrote "La Laitière et le Pot au lait." Collinet, on the other hand, finds excellent reasons to reverse the order of composition. Why would La Fontaine be interested in this *fait divers*, while excluding all other *faits divers*, if he were not already contemplating a structure that would give sense to this anecdote? Collinet wisely concludes that the problem probably does not have an objective solution: "[...] les deux fables coexistent, l'une sortie des livres, l'autre de la vie, fondant si bien la vérité et la fiction qu'il est devenu impossible de déceler le secret de leur mélange" (*Le Monde littéraire* 213). Whatever the order of their historical composition, within the order given the fables constituting Book 7 of the *Fables,* "La Laitière et le Pot au lait" is placed first in order to play the role of textual generator from which "Le Curé et le Mort" seems to derive its structure, sense, and language. The two critical approaches that seek to unknot the historical relation between the two texts assume that the fable's doubleness must imply on some level a guest and host relationship. For Collinet, "La Laitière" provides meaning and structure against which "Le Curé" can be built; for the editors of the Pléiade, "Le Curé" provided the author with a plot that led eventually to the discovery of its already written double.

There may be difficulties in unknotting the historical web that binds these two fables, but we are very well informed on the facts of the case, on the literary history of "Le Curé et le Mort," its history as text, and its textualization as *histoire*, since both the anecdote and the reception of the fable are recounted by the incomparable Mme de Sévigné. Mme de Sévigné closes her letter of February 26, 1672, to Mme de Grignan, which Roger Duchêne likens to a "rapide gazette" (*Correspondance* 1: 1239), with a feigned disparagement of the day's news: "Je vous mandai tant de choses en dernier lieu qu'il me semble que je n'ai rien à dire aujourd'hui." Here are two of the leftovers she finds to report:

> M. de Boufflers a tué un homme, après sa mort. Il était dans sa bière et en carrosse. On le menait à une lieue de Boufflers, pour l'enterrer; son curé était avec le corps. On verse; la bière coupe le cou au pauvre curé. Hier, un homme versa en revenant de Saint-Germain; il se creva le cœur, et mourut dans le carrosse. (*Correspondance* 1: 446)

M. de Boufflers's curious story will be echoed in La Fontaine's fable; the second story recounted, lacking a named protagonist and any piquancy of detail, might never have been told, were it not for the sensational story of M. de Boufflers and his curé. In Mme de Sévigné's letter, the extraordinary death caused by M. de Boufflers, which inverts the stereotyped situation "the curé buries the dead," is counterbalanced by the commonplace accident.

In his essay on the "Structure du fait divers" (*Essais* 188-97), Roland Barthes evaluates the paradoxical nature of the *fait divers* that makes of it literature almost *avant la lettre*:

> Causalité aléatoire, coïncidence ordonnée, c'est à la jonction de ces deux mouvements que se constitue le fait divers: tous deux finissent en effet par recouvrir une zone ambiguë *où l'événement est pleinement vécu*

comme un signe dont le contenu est cependant incertain. (196-97; Barthes's emphasis)

The *fait divers*, the unusual events surrounding the death of M. de Boufflers's curé as recounted by Mme de Sévigné, is rendered interesting in that a stereotyped, ritualized situation is inverted. The anecdote seems to mean something, but what? The sense of this accident is strictly undecidable, or rather the sense is, or could be, Barthes's paradox: "Causalité aléatoire, coïncidence ordonnée." A later Barthes might have concluded that it is by the multiplication of such stories that the paradoxicality of the *fait divers* re-enters the realm of *doxa*. Mme de Sévigné chooses to attenuate the strangeness of her first anecdote by doubling it with a second, unambiguously banal accident. La Fontaine proceeds differently, as we have seen, by substituting *histoire* for history. In both cases however, the macabre story seems to require a double, whether, as Mme de Sévigné would have it, to reassure her reader that M. de Boufflers's story is probably only an accident, or in La Fontaine's case, to integrate it into a larger context, giving it a wider sense and scope than this meager story seems capable of sustaining.

***

"La Laitière et le Pot au lait" is in some senses already a double fable in that two stories are told, that of Perrette and that of the narrator. First, Perrette's story is told directly without narratorial intervention. At the end of the story proper, an editorial note places Perrette's story within a certain literary, or rather paraliterary, tradition:

> Le récit en farce en fut fait;
> On l'appela *le Pot au lait*.

According to the narrator, the fable we have just read is a retelling of a farce. There is no reason not to believe the narrator regarding the textual source of the fable despite the fact that no one, including Mme de Sévigné, seems to have heard of it.[6] The point here is first of all that the fable is explicitly represented as having a literary source and, second, that this source belongs to the low style of popular comedy.

The second part of the fable, the narrator's personal revery, takes the place of

Bodies and Souls

an explicit *moralité*. This second part of the fable consists of two major movements. It first generalizes the milkmaid's propensity to daydream into a universal human phenomenon and then, *mutatis mutandis*, repeats her story in the first person. "Le Curé et le Mort," the second fable in this diptych, retells Perrette's story in darker tones. The curé plays the role of Perrette; the corpse he is about to lay to rest, that of the pot of milk. The fable ends with this curious *moralité*:

> Proprement toute notre vie;
> Est le curé Chouart, qui sur son mort comptait,
> Et la fable du *Pot au lait*.

The *moralité* of "Le Curé" thus explicitly refers to its double by quoting the title, which is also the title of the "farce" from which the La Fontaine's fable purportedly derives. One is struck by the extraordinary bookishness in the way the two fables refer to each other and to the mysterious farce. The fables explicitly assert their own textuality and intertextuality while thematically englobing life and death, comedy and tragedy, body and soul.

The relation between these two fables is, of course, not limited to thematic parallels and this incidence of self-reference. An elaborate network of echoes and correspondences articulates the texts of "La Laitière et le Pot au lait" and "Le Curé et le Mort." In these fables, there are seven common codes that enrich and problematize the relation between these two texts, these double fables.[7] These are the corporeal code, to which are linked by synecdoche the vestimentary and the erotic codes, the animal code, the onomastic code, the social code, and the literary code, to which I have already alluded and to which I will inevitably return.

Least evident in these two fables is the animal code, the code on which the fable as a genre depends. In fables in which the protagonists are human, the animal code serves as a generic marker, a reminder that the text at hand is a fable, and, conversely, opens the text in other directions. La Fontaine's famous "definition" of the royal court, for example ("Peuple *caméléon*, peuple *singe* du maître" ["Les Obsèques de la Lionne," *Fables* 8.14]), depends on the existence of the fable as a genre for the full effect of these animal metaphors. Similarly, the shepherd in "Les Animaux malades de la peste" (*Fables* 7.1) is "[. . .] de ces gens-là qui sur les animaux / Se font un *chimérique* empire." The adjective *chimérique* of course means illusory, but in a fable must recall the three-headed dog of the underworld, an animal otherwise lacking in La Fontaine's bestiary. By contrast, the animal code in "La Laitière" seems to function simply as the inscription of an economic system. Animals in "La Laitière" seem to be no more than the mere equivalent of money, which also comes into play along the way:

> Notre laitière ainsi troussée
> Comptait déjà dans sa pensée
> Tout le prix de son lait, en employait l'argent [. . .].

Perrette's investments have already got her a pig, which also can be transformed into money: "J'aurai le revendant de l'argent bel et bon." The scandal of "Le Curé" is, of course, that the human body can be converted into cash in much the same way as can Perrette's imaginary menagerie. A very minor detail does, however, open a perspective toward the fable genre:

> Le Renard sera bien habile,
> S'il ne m'en [= chickens] laisse assez pour avoir un cochon.

The fox in a fable is always a potential character, no more or no less important than human protagonists. This potential is, of course, not realized in this fable. As we will see, in "Le Curé" the animal code makes its appearance in the name of the protagonist.

If the animal world is only suggested in these fables, the human world is represented in its three traditional social states. Each character is clearly linked to a social class. Perrette belongs to the peasantry and Jean Chouart to the clergy, while "Gros-Jean," the narrator of the revery, aspires to the nobility in his dreams of grandeur. The social elevation of the narrator is, in this respect, interesting. We discover the point of transition between the body of the fable and its soul, the narrator's meditation, in two juxtaposed proverbial expressions whose sense is identical. The difference resides in their language. The first recalls the countryside, symbolic space of the peasantry; the second, the noble's *châteaux*:

> Quel esprit ne bat la campagne?
> Qui ne fait châteaux en Espagne?

The universality of daydreaming is signaled by citing the example of two kings (Pichrocole and Pyrrhus) along with the milkmaid, while the narrator's *folie des grandeurs* is expressed in "noble" terms:

Bodies and Souls 49

> Quand je suis seul, je fais au plus brave un défi;
> Je m'écarte, je vais détrôner le Sophi;
> On m'élit roi, mon peuple m'aime;
> Les diadèmes vont sur ma tête pleuvant [...].

Finally, I would like to turn to what might be called the corporeal code, body language, to which are linked by synecdoche the vestimentary and the erotic codes.

***

In the beginning there is Perrette, the milkmaid:

> Perrette sur sa tête ayant un Pot au lait
> Bien posé sur un coussinet,
> Prétendait arriver sans encombre à la ville.
> Légère et court vêtue elle allait à grands pas;
> Ayant mis ce jour-là, pour être plus agile,
> Cotillon simple, et souliers plats.

The body of Perrette as it is drawn in these first verses is simply bipolar; "Perrette" is not described from head to feet; she is nothing but head and legs. The first verse names one pole, the head, strategically placed at the caesura where its phonic substance echoes the name of the protagonist (/peRɛt/—/tɛːt/) while its etymology points forward to *pot* (*tête* < *testa*, "pot"). The jug is balanced on the head, where the contiguity of jug and head establishes a metonymic system of relations.[8] This play will further develop as Perrette's head will be seen to contain thought in much the same way as the jug contains milk, soon to be transmuted in Perrette's mind into eggs, chickens, and so on. At the other extreme, legs dominate: *court vêtue, cotillon simple, souliers plats*. These vestimentary details are evoked for their contiguity to the unnamed legs and feet of the milkmaid, while occluding them, preventing them from having to be named. The "body" of Perrette as traced in this fable resembles a sort of graphism, a figure of lines, or points, in which semantic bundles mark the head and the legs. In this, Perrette somewhat resembles the heron of "Le Héron—La Fille" (*Fables* 7.4), a three-lined diagram marked for movement, a vector of uncertain direction:

> Un jour, sur ses longs pieds, allait je ne sais où,
> Le Héron au long bec emmanché d'un long cou.

The problem in "La Laitière et le Pot au lait" is that in this diagram there is no *trait d'union*, no contact sketched between poles. The head-pot goes its own way, accumulating, amassing weight and volume as one animal is bartered against the next, ignorant of the destabilizing effect at the other end.

In "Le Curé," vestimentary details first of all delineate the body of the deceased:

> Notre défunt était en carrosse porté,
>   Bien et dûment empaqueté,
> Et vêtu d'une robe, hélas! qu'on nomme bière,
>   Robe d'hiver, robe d'été,
> Que les morts ne dépouillent guère.

At the other end of the spectrum, clothing enters the revery of the curé just at its apogee as he calculates what the price of the funeral will get him. Here again clothing is meant to reveal more than it hides:

> Il fondait là-dessus l'achat d'une feuillette
>   Du meilleur vin des environs;
>   Certaine nièce assez propette
>   Et sa chambrière Pâquette
>   Devaient avoir des cotillons.

The gift of *cotillons* for niece and chambermaid enters the series of the curé's little pleasures in life, thus acquiring a certain erotic potential within the text.[9] Both Eros and Thanatos come fully clothed in this fable.

The coincidence of proper names in these two fables is also rather pointed. The form of the name of the chambermaid, *Pâquette*, as well as of the unique attribute of the niece, *propette*, easily recalls *Perrette*, who, it will be remembered, also wore a *cotillon*, but for reasons otherwise utilitarian. Fragonard's well-known illustration of Perrette's accident (an engraving of which is reproduced in ed. Couton, *Fables* interleaf 190-91) takes full advantage of the erotic potential of this article of dress, and reveals in Fragonard a better reader of La Fontaine than he might ordinarily be considered. Clothing is a powerful textual metaphor that functions in this fable as a veil, a protection against

Bodies and Souls 51

unwelcome eyes (Fragonard notwithstanding), and as metonym for the body beneath, the unspeakable corpse or the curé's object of desire. I will have occasion to examine in greater detail in Chapter 7, "Reading (through) the Veil," La Fontaine's use of this striking figure of his text.

Two other names echo each other in our two fables. The disembodied narrator's fall from his exalted state of revery is represented as an act of self-naming:

> Quelque accident fait-il que je rentre en moi-même;
> Je suis gros Jean/Gros-Jean comme devant.[10]

Commentators have been quick to remind us that this narrator shares a Christian name with the author of the *Fables*. He also shares a name with the curé, who, unlike the anonymous corpse, has a proper name.[11] The fable insists on this proper name, Jean Chouart, by repeating it three times. There are good reasons why it should so insist; the textual strands I have been tracing between these two fables are knotted here. First of all, the curé is called Jean, like Jean de La Fontaine, like "Gros-Jean," it is true, but also like Jean Lapin (*Fables* 2.8 and 7.15) or any number of other Jeans in the *Fables*. Couton quotes Furetière to remind us that in the language, *Jean* is not only a proper name designating individuals but also a "nom propre que le peuple a mis en usage dans la langue, en le joignant abusivement à plusieurs mots injurieux" (Furetière, *Jean*).[12] It was perhaps this propensity of the word *Jean* to enter into combinations with other terms that motivated the first literary use of *Jean Chouart*, not by La Fontaine but by Rabelais. In *Pantagruel,* Jean Chouart is the name Panurge gives the contents of his codpiece: "Tenez (montrant sa longue braguette) voicy maistre Jean Chouart qui demande logis" (qtd. in ed. Couton, *Fables* 474). The use of clothing as a verbal euphemism for the unmentionable body is curiously mirrored in the Rabelaisian intertext.

For readers who miss the Rabelaisian allusion in the curé's name, *Jean Chouart* is readable in another way, too. A *chouart* is an animal, more precisely a predatory bird, the male of the *chouette*. This fact adds interest to the first verse in which the curé is called by name: "Messire Jean Chouart couvait des yeux son mort." The figurative expression "couvait des yeux" regains some of its properness when the proper name of the subject is the name of a bird, even a male bird. Perhaps the curé's nest egg will resemble in fecundity the "triple couvée" of Perrette's imaginary chickens.

Perrette's dream is not destined to be realized, but, curiously enough, her misfortune here is in some respects the result of poetic imitation, a play on words. At the height of her revery, she imagines herself watching

> [. . .] une vache et son veau,
> Que je verrai sauter au milieu du troupeau[.]
> Perrette là-dessus saute aussi, transportée.

Her body imitates the movement of her imaginary cattle; her spiritual *transports* become absolutely physical, and her pot of milk obeys the law of gravity. Head and legs, soul and body, conspire in Perrette's downfall:

> Le lait tombe; adieu veau, vache, cochon, couvée.

The curé's accident is less neatly motivated. He has just arrived at *cotillons* for his niece and Pâquette:

> Sur cette agréable pensée
> Un heurt survient, adieu le char.

The curé's accident seems entirely coincidental. Why, in the order of things, should the accident arrive just now? "Causalité aléatoire, coïncidence ordonnée" (Barthes). "La Laitière" and "Le Curé" provide two models of the accidental fall that are curiously juxtaposed in the narrator's restaging of the story.

Unlike Perrette and the curé, the narrator of the second part of "La Laitière" is not represented as a body, a character in a scene, but as a disembodied voice. The narrator's meditation in praise of revery is almost an *antimoralité* in that it contradicts the easily supplied and therefore, I suppose, easily supplanted warning against not tending to business. In place of the expected *moralité*, the soul of the fable, souls play a role:

> Chacun songe en veillant, il n'est rien de plus doux:
> Une flatteuse erreur emporte alors nos âmes.

This verse relentlessly repeats *âme*, etymologically *anima*, "breath," carried away by a *flatteuse* (by false etymology from *flare*, "to blow")[13] *erreur* (AIR-eur). A less detailed reading of this verse would no doubt be carried along by its music, especially the repetitions of /R/. Breath (*anima*) is inscribed in the phonic substance of this wonderful verse.

Bodies and Souls

Unfortunately for those who would hear in this section of the fable the authentic voice of our poet, this daydream is scarcely more distinguished than Perrette's, even if it is written in the "noble" mode. The narrator's dreams of conquest and dominion simply parody those of any two-bit Matamore. But this dream too will come to an end, leaving behind the name of our narrator: "Je suis Gros-Jean/gros Jean comme devant."

Our reading of Perrette's and the curé's catastrophes have provided us with a model that will allow us to question the nature of the cause whose effect is the end of the narrator's revery. The apogee of the daydreamer's glory is expressed in a baroque image Corneille might not have disdained[14] ("Les diadèmes vont sur ma tête pleuvant"), immediately followed by the return to reality ("Quelque accident fait-il que je rentre en moi-même [. . .]"). Note that in this case, as in the two others, an accident is necessary to bring the daydream to an end. The etymology of accident (from *cadere,* via *accidere,* "to fall") might serve to link the abstract "quelque accident" to the concrete and burlesque image of diadems raining down. "Les diadèmes vont sur ma tête pleuvant" is readable both in the figurative mode as the height of the daydream and in the literal mode as the "accident" that will bring the daydreamer to his senses. Our narrator, however disembodied has been his voice, in these verses is shown to have a head that, it seems, is not only a container for pure reflection. Like Perrette's story that according to the narrator was made into a farce, this second story, that of the megalomaniac daydreamer, may easily, abusively some will claim, be made into a farce if readers consent to read the literal and proper at the expense of the figurative. These closing verses of "La Laitière" thus maintain a delicate balance between the abstraction of intellectual discourse ("quelque accident") and low, physical comedy. The poem maintains both readings in equilibrium while reminding us one more time that every *sens figuré* has a *sens propre* and every soul, a body.

As we have seen, the fall from the heights of revery is expressed in the final verse of the fable as signature:

> Je suis gros Jean comme devant.
>
> (ed. Couton, *Fables*)

or

> Je suis Gros-Jean comme devant.
>
> (ed. Pléiade)

Just who is this narrator who names himself here? Or rather, how should his name be written? Should we read "gros," a corporeal, material attribute of "Jean," of Jean de La Fontaine, perhaps? In this case the name and its attribute serve as a reminder that "Jean" is not only a voice but a body as well. Or shall we read "Gros-Jean," a unique proper name, which denotes a fictive character not to be confused with "Jean Chouart" or "Jean Lapin"?[15] This problem of interpretation, like the unresolved textual problem of the writing of the name of the narrator, is strictly ambiguous. La Fontaine's editors nonetheless have had to choose leaving the meaning of this signature hanging in the balance.

The double fables of "La Laitière et le Pot au lait" and "Le Curé et le Mort" seem to tell one more time the story of the inscription of difference, the inscription of a privileged interiority (the daydream, the errant soul, the disembodied voice) and parasitical exteriority (the body, the accident). From within this system emerges another, the conjugation of propriety, the proper name, and property (Perrette's animals; the curé's wine and women; Gros-Jean's kingdoms). This search for the proper in all of its manifestations is made explicit in the moral that closes "Le Curé et le Mort":

Proprement [my emphasis] toute notre vie;
Est le curé Chouart, qui sur son mort comptait,
Et la fable du *Pot au lait.*

4
Making the Difference: Textuality and Sexuality

"Les Deux Pigeons"

Readers approach a fable first and perhaps above all as a text to be interpreted. Taken only as a story, the fable does not mean enough to satisfy readers' desire for textual fulfillment. Mature readers know that there is something "in" the fable that must be gotten "out" of it. The fable as a genre is indelibly marked by this hermeneutical imperative. Interpretation of the fable takes place according to well-known rules. At least partially coded analogies link the animal world of the fable to the human world. The finality of the fable is precisely the point that it makes about us: *De nobis fabula narratur.* Conventional expectations about the necessity of interpreting the fable in a certain way limit the full range and play of possible readings. However, as we have seen in "Démocrite et les Abdéritains," La Fontaine's fables in certain cases refuse to allow naturalization through reference to a coded and closed system of analogies to the human world. The center fails to hold, and the text produces, in spite of readers' best efforts, more meanings than a single, anthropomorphizing interpretation can accommodate. The fundamental relation which dictates how the fable means itself to be read is no longer analogy but anomaly.

This anomalous, abnormal relation seems to me to be no where more evident than in La Fontaine's "Les Deux Pigeons" (*Fables* 9.2). A universally admired masterpiece, "Les Deux Pigeons" has found its way into every anthology. Yet if one reads the commentary that three centuries have inscribed in the margins of this poem, one is struck by a certain uneasiness, a critical impatience with the story of the two pigeons themselves, and a distinct effort to oblige the fable to conform to the elegiac (human) finale: "Amants, heureux amants [...]."[1] The point I will be making is that, in this instance, the apologue and the narrator's personal meditation that supplants the moral in the way we observed in "La Laitière et le Pot au lait" are radically disproportionate, anomalous. What I will be calling the anomaly of "Les Deux Pigeons" is first of all a question of the grammatical gender, and therefore by analogy, of the sexual roles of the two pigeons. Readers' perception of anomaly depends, of course, on a fundamental rule of the fable genre: Animal characters adopt the sexual roles of their grammatical gender.[2] Occasionally, the language fails to supply both a masculine and feminine form for every animal that could be a fable character. French, for example, gives only the masculine for *renard*, *léopard*, and *éléphant*; only the feminine for *cigale* and *fourmi*. In such cases related species may be linguistically coupled. *Crapaud/grenouille*, *pigeon/colombe* and *rat/souris* come to mind. In "La Souris métamorphosée en fille" (*Fables* 9.7), for example, the word *rat* awakens the metamorphosized *souris* to her true nature:

> Au mot de Rat, la Damoiselle [la souris]
> Ouvrit l'oreille; il fut l'époux.

The point is that the fabulist disposes of various tricks of the trade for naturalizing the tale of the two pigeons as a love story. However, in "Les Deux Pigeons," the two pigeons call each other "brother" three times in the fable; the voyaging pigeon changes gender along the way and the apologue ends with an invocation to lovers: "Amants, heureux amants, voulez-vous voyager?" Exactly that information that would allow readers to crack the code, to satisfy their desire to know the "true" (that is, human) relation between the two pigeons and thereby to learn something about love itself (the ostensible signified), is withheld or repressed. Nevertheless, in order to make any sense at all of this story, readers are obliged to cast the sexual roles of the two pigeons at every moment in their reading of the fable.[3] They must interpret and watch their interpretations be frustrated at every step of the way.

***

> Deux Pigeons s'aimaient d'amour tendre.

Two pigeons, the emblem of love itself, love each other mutually, tenderly. The two pigeons are first of all an archetypal symbol, a culturally motivated sign signifying "love." They are truly hieroglyphics in the sense I explored in Chapter 1. On the level of pure symbolism, this first verse is thus overcoded to the point of tautology, since it merely translates the sense of the hieroglyphic. But this state of eternal and blissful signification cannot last. While animals in La Fontaine's fables may very well have been chosen for their symbolic value, they can at any moment become characters in a tale. La Fontaine's fables depend precisely on this tension between two signifying systems, the symbolic and the representational. The way these competing modes of signification are displayed in the text of the fable is particularly interesting for the theory of the text in the seventeenth century. In Chapter 1, I considered the paradoxical process by which a "scene," supposedly the representation of an action in the world, was read as a hieroglyphic. In this chapter, I would like to examine how the hieroglyphic, the archetypal couple, is deconstructed by founding a difference (where in the realm of pure symbol there ought not to be one), but *not* the difference that would allow readers to naturalize the pigeons' story simply as a human love story. As potential characters, the two pigeons are in the first verse perfectly indistinguishable. They are of the same species and of the same grammatical gender. Their love is identical ("tendre") and reciprocal ("s'aimaient"). In short, there is no difference. Their story will be precisely about making a difference.

The pigeons' story takes place in two moments. It begins with a dialogue between the two pigeons and ends with the voyage and return of one of the pigeons. Before the decisive voyage itself takes place, each pigeon speaks his piece. The pigeons' discourses are transcribed in the fable as represented speech and, in a sense, they are nothing but pure voice. However, their speeches imbed a number of echoes of other voices or, rather, citations of other texts. At the center of each pigeon's discourse is a maxim, the unsigned quotation of everyone and no one, which in the seventeenth century guaranteed motivational *vraisemblance*.[4] The stay-at-home pigeon cites the maxim "L'absence est le plus grand des maux," and the voyager counters with another: "Quiconque ne voit guère / N'a guère à dire aussi." These maxims are not the only citations in the fable; La Fontaine's fable imbeds other texts as well, texts that do not make good bedfellows in that the anomalousness of "Les Deux Pigeons" can be seen in the collation of incompatible texts partially cited in the fable.

The most obvious citation is, of course, Pilpay's fable, La Fontaine's source (qtd. in ed. Régnier 2: 512-15). Pilpay's allegorizing nomenclature—the pigeons are called the Lover and the Loved One (Aimant and Aimé)—imposes a grammatical and thematic structure (active/passive) on Pilpay's fable that runs counter to La Fontaine's insistence on reciprocity and identity. A more interesting example is found in Horace's allusion to the fable in his epistle to Fuscus:

> Vrbis amatorem Fuscum salvere iubemus
> ruris amatores, hac in re scilicet una
> multum dissimiles, at cetera paene gemelli
> fraternis animis—quidquid negat alter et alter—
> adnuimus pariter vetuli notique columbi.
> tu nidum servas; ego laudo ruris amoeni
> rivos [. . .].
>
> (*Epistularum Lib.* 1.10.1-7)

Two male characters this time, almost like brothers ("gemelli / fraternis animis," the possible generator of "frère" in the fable). The other (*tu*) is the stay-at-home pigeon; the poet (*ego*) casts himself in the role of the voyager. And then there is Vergil's couple Aeneas and Dido. It is Dido's voice one hears in the discourse of the stay-at-home pigeon:

> L'absence est le plus grand des maux:
> Non pas pour vous, cruel. [. . .]
>
> quin etiam hiberno moliris sidere classem,
> et mediis properas aquilonibus ire per altum,
> crudelis! [. . .]
>
> (*Aeneid* 4.309-11)

I will let Leo Spitzer take responsibility for casting the roles: "[. . .] the reminiscences of Vergil's Dido which are found in the discourse of the pigeon who remains behind (vv. 7-11) cannot be explained unless one admits that La Fontaine saw this speaker *as a woman*" ("Nota" 87; my translation; Spitzer's emphasis).

Once again, La Fontaine's fable reveals itself as an intertextual practice, a reading of other texts within the text of the fable.[5] "Les Deux Pigeons" is not just one (more) discourse "about" love or friendship, but a collation of incompatible discourses about love which do not add up to a single unambiguous truth. More than being "about" love in any fixed, analogical, anthropomorphic

Making the Difference   59

sense, the fable of the two pigeons may be about its anomalies, inconsistencies, and disproportions, or to use a more positive-sounding word, its texture. In any case, what seems to me most striking in this fable is that the sexuality of the two pigeons, the way their respective roles must be cast at a given moment in the fable, is inextricably linked to the intertextuality of the fable. The allegory of love in "Les Deux Pigeons" is also the allegory of the reading of the fable.

The pretext for the second pigeon's voyage is to have a story to tell. He represents his voyage as a quest for a content whose form he states abstractly: "J'étais là; telle chose m'avint; / Vous y croirez être vous-même." His story has, however, already been told, predicted, by the other pigeon. It is interesting in this respect that the source of the pigeon's information on the story level betrays one of the characteristic ambiguities of this fable: "[. . .] Un corbeau / Tout à l'heure annonçait malheur à quelque oiseau." The verse is ambiguous in that readers cannot construct a single naturalizing fiction to determine whether a passing raven told the story of the voyaging pigeon or whether the raven itself is a sign, a sign written in nature, of the pigeon's misfortunes.[6] The dialectic of the (represented as) written and the (represented as) spoken pervades the poem at every level. This dialectic will become our principal concern in the following chapter on *Les Amours de Psyché et de Cupidon*.

The voyage of the second pigeon, or rather the story he will have to tell, is already encapsulated in the predictions of the first pigeon. These predictions provide a matrix to be expanded in the actual voyage of the pigeon. His adventures in the second part of the fable do seem, *mutatis mutandis*, to follow the program announced in the other pigeon's predictions.[7] The predicted "faucons" appear in their hyperbolic avatars "vautour" and "aigle." The rain ("Hélas, dirai-je, il pleut") becomes an "orage"; "réseaux" corresponds to "las." In much the same way, the simple pleasures of domestic life ("bon soupé, bon gîte") are reduced to the barest of minimums. Instead of a "bon gîte," "un seul arbre s'offrit"; for his "soupé," "du blé répandu," which, we will see, hides more than one trap. Every element in the first pigeon's predictions is hyperbolically transformed in the second pigeon's voyage, while the semantically relevant features that allow readers to make the necessary connections are retained.

One element does, however, seem to trouble this smooth, analogical relation between the first pigeon's predictions and their fulfillment in the actual voyage of the second pigeon:

> Mon frère a-t-il tout ce qu'il veut,
> Bon soupé, bon gîte et le reste?

"Quelle grâce, quelle finesse sous-entendues dans ce petit mot et le reste [. . .]!" exclaims Chamfort (qtd. in ed. Régnier 2: 362n). Spitzer translates more directly: "We must understand *et le reste* as erotic pleasure and the wife's preoccupation with the probable lack, during the voyage, of what she could give is a moving touch in this transposition into the world of animals" ("Nota" 87; my translation). Of course, the reader is under no obligation to accept either Spitzer's particular casting of the stay-at-home pigeon as the voyaging pigeon's wife or, for that matter, his assumption that a single variety of human love has simply been transposed into an animal allegory. Régnier's interpretation that the pigeons are not lovers at all but two male friends would not necessarily be contradictory at this point in the text. In "Les Deux Amis" (*Fables* 8.11) for example, the true friend cares about the erotic life of his friend:

> [. . .] Vous ennuyez-vous point
> De coucher toujours seul? Une esclave assez belle
> Etait à mes côtés: voulez-vous qu'on l'appelle?

Readers of this fable have little trouble, it seems, finding a meaning for "et le reste." The phrase, although attenuated, falls neatly into a series whose dominant feature is physical comfort or pleasure. In spite of the essential ambiguity of the exact nature of the two pigeons' roles, erotic love nevertheless emerges as a structural, or rather textural, element in the fable and therefore, if our model holds, should reappear in the second pigeon's voyage. This textual strand of latent eroticism does in fact resurface in the pigeon's voyage in a manner that further alerts readers to the functioning of the whole text.

> Dans un champ à l'écart voit du blé répandu,
> Voit un pigeon auprès; cela lui donne envie:
> Il y vole, il est pris: ce blé couvrait d'un las,
> Les menteurs et traîtres appas.

On the story level, the pigeon, after having more or less successfully weathered the storm, sees another pigeon and grain spread on the ground. The grain and the pigeon turn out to be lures for a trap.[8] Readers might already be struck by the syntactic parallelism between the *blé* and the lure-pigeon which extends in both cases to the ellipsis of the pronoun subject of *voit*, and by the

Making the Difference 61

ambiguity of *cela*'s antecedent. This syntactic legerdemain renders *envie* ambiguous as well: What exactly does the pigeon want? Food, we think. "Bon soupé" certainly, "et le reste"? But it is "les menteurs et traîtres appas" that alters the mimetic functioning of the passage while enlarging its signification to encompass the repressed element (erotic love) readers read into "et le reste." I see at work here a kind of pun that Michael Riffaterre has called an intertextual syllepsis.[9] In this case the syllepsis depends on the confusion, or rather fusion, of two originally different words. *Appas* designates, according to Littré, the "beautés qui dans une femme excitent le désir." This word was often (con-)fused in the seventeenth century with the plural of *appât*, "bait." Littré cites "Les Deux Pigeons" to prove that this confusion between *appas* and *appâts* "n'est qu'une affaire d'orthographe" (Littré, *appas*). Of course, it is much more than that here. The contextual sense may very well be *appâts*; the intertextual sense is *appas*. The intertextual reading of this passage is confirmed by the double pertinence of the epithets "les menteurs et traîtres appas," whose sense links this moment in the pigeon's voyage to the *topos* of conventional literary misogyny. The anteposition of the epithets, common in the high style with *appas*, gives a literary ring to the verse, which makes the syllepsis perceptible to readers.[10]

Representation of the pigeons as characters in the *récit*, we have seen, takes place in three moments. First the symbolic couple is deconstructed by founding a difference: the two pigeons speak, that is, they are represented in the text as voices. One voice tells, predicts, the unhappy story of his partner. Curiously enough, this story has already been told, or rather written in natural signs (the raven) or in dreams as yet undreamed ("Je ne songerai plus [. . .]"). The stated purpose of the second pigeon's voyage is to find a voice, to have a story to tell. The pigeon's story is then actualized as the hyperbolic coming-true of the first pigeon's predictions. However, if the pigeons were represented in the first part of the fable as voices, the voyaging pigeon is now represented as body. The pigeon acquires a body in the text, that is, the parts of his body are cited, as his body is disfigured in the course of his adventures. Each of his adventures leaves its mark on the pigeon:

> [. . .] il part tout morfondu,
> Sèche du mieux qu'il peut son corps chargé de pluie.
>
> Le las était usé! si bien que de son aile,
> De ses pieds, de son bec, l'oiseau le rompt enfin.
> Quelque plume y périt.

The pigeon's story, already predicted, is now inscribed on the body of the pigeon. The pigeon's story and the pigeon's body have become one, consubstantial.[11] A comparable episode of corporeal fragmentation occurs in the early chapters of *L'Astrée*. Céladon, convinced that Astrée can never love him, attempts suicide by throwing himself into the river. His body washes ashore in time to be found by Galathée and her nymphs:

> mais le voyant de plus près, elle [Galathée] le crut mort, car il avait encore les jambes en l'eau, le bras droit mollement étendu par-dessus la tête, la gauche à demi tourné par derrière, et comme engagé sous le corps. Le cou faisait un pli en avant pour la pesanteur de la tête qui se laissait aller en arrière, la bouche à demi entrouverte et presque pleine de sablon, dégouttait encore de tous côtés; le visage en quelques lieux égratigné et souillé [. . .]. (Urfé 33-34)

Dalia Judovitz's commentary on this passage is revealing: "Rather than being perceived as a whole, the body becomes a hieroglyph, a series of discontinuous signs written by nature as a consequence of having been marked by love" (533). In "Les Deux Pigeons" this aspect of the inscription is more pronounced in that each of the marks is a sign of a particular adventure, recounted in the narration as well as in the predictions of the other pigeon. The body of the pigeon is in this sense a more fully elaborated text than the body of Céladon. In *L'Astrée* the discovery of Céladon's mutilated body was made possible because the scene had already been pre-represented visually in the nymphs' magic mirror. In "Les Deux Pigeons" the pre-representation took place in the predictions of the stay-at-home pigeon and, outside of the narrative, in the speaking (or writing) of the raven.

Before the pigeon can return home, one last chapter needs to be written:

> Mais un fripon d'enfant, cet âge est sans pitié,
> Prit sa fronde et, du coup, tua plus d'à moitié
> La volatile malheureuse,
> Qui, maudissant sa curiosité,
> Traînant l'aile et tirant le pié,
> Demi-morte et demi-boiteuse,
> Droit au logis s'en retourna.
> Que bien, que mal, *elle* arriva [my emphasis]
> Sans autre aventure fâcheuse.

Making the Difference 63

If one reads this passage, as I believe is necessary, with an eye toward casting the pigeon's role, one notices that the pigeon is designated by the periphrasis *volatile malheureuse*, which in this fable is grammatically feminine. Seventeenth-century dictionaries, however, are not in agreement on the spelling, meaning, or gender of the word.[12] Whether the word means in its etymological purity "any animal that flies" or in its barnyard sense "a bird that is good to eat," the irony of the periphrasis is apparent—and cruel. The pigeon can scarcely walk, much less fly, and the fact of his being good to eat hardly justifies his being the butt of so much active malevolence. In any case, the use of the periphrasis *volatile malheureuse*, the corresponding feminine adjectives *demi-morte et demi-boiteuse*, and the pronoun *elle* seems to have transformed the pigeon into a female character.

On one level, of course, this sexual-grammatical metamorphosis, itself a scandal, obviates the greater scandal of sexually untypable pigeons in what passes for a love story. The analogical relation between the grammatical gender of the animal name and a sexual role in the human world is not a given in this fable; it is a by-product of the functioning of the text. La Fontaine's pigeons are not merely examples from a zoological treatise, pure hieroglyphics signifying love, or, for that matter, human characters transposed into birds; they are ultimately and radically textual figures. Just as each adventure left its mark on the voyaging pigeon, the last, most devastating adventure inscribes femininity on the pigeon. The fable is readable as a love story because the pigeon, having become the text of her adventures, is readable as a female character.

The apologue proper closes with a tag line familiar to readers of the *contes*. The narrator pulls the curtain, so to speak, on a scene his feigned modesty will not allow him to describe, and readers are left with the responsibility for deciding exactly what will take place:

> Voilà nos gens rejoints; et je laisse à juger
> De combien de plaisirs ils payèrent leurs peines.

At this point, once the pigeon has been transformed into a feminine pronoun ("elle arriva"), *plaisirs* can safely be understood as sensual, erotic pleasure. A meaning the anomalies of the text have kept some readers and critics from admitting too freely can now be admitted and even seen as a transition (in the sense Spitzer gives the word) to the human finale where it is unambiguously a question of a man's love for a woman. This naturalization has been bought at a considerable price to the pigeons. On the story level, the pigeon has been dismembered, the signs of her adventures inscribed on her body. But "Les Deux Pigeons" has a happy ending. In the end, it is the prediction of the voyaging pigeon that comes true: "Mon voyage dépeint / Vous sera d'un plaisir extrême." Sensual pleasure and the pleasure of the story have become metaphors one for the other.

If, as Jules Brody has suggested, "our critical vocabularies, like all language, are hopelessly, helplessly metaphoric before they are either concrete or abstract" (80-81), there is perhaps another sense to La Fontaine's "definition" of the fable we examined in the previous chapter. "Les Deux Pigeons" simultaneously allegorizes and deconstructs the founding metaphor of La Fontaine's poetic project. As potential moralists, readers are supposed to be interested primarily in the "soul" of the fable, its *anima*, the breath of the word as it gives life to the inert body of the animals, of the text itself. The fable of the two pigeons as an allegory of its own reading and writing inverts this hierarchical order. The body, the text, and their pleasures are in the end valorized. Marc Fumaroli is certainly right when he calls "Les Deux Pigeons" the "résumé de toute l'entreprise poétique et sapientiale des *Fables*" (*Fables* 2: 360). This fable is also, I would claim, an elegant resumé of the fable's textuality.

5
Inscribing the Voice: Oral Performance and the Written Text

Les Amours de Psyché et de Cupidon

Les Amours de Psyché et de Cupidon (1669) is La Fontaine's longest and most elaborate single work. In some ways, it is his chrestomathy of seventeenth-century styles and genres ranging from the fairy tale to the Platonic dialogue, and including examples of literary and conversational prose as well as descriptive and lyric poetry. In other ways, it seems to be his *nouveau roman* in that it involves a highly original and unusual self-reflexive exchange between a framing narrative and an included tale. Jean-Pierre Collinet, perhaps reflecting on the double edge of La Fontaine's often avowed purpose in writing (to instruct and to please), has called *Psyché* variously an "art of reading" and a "hymn to the pleasure of reading" ("L'Art de lire" 94, 95). Although this aspect of La Fontaine's novel has rarely been studied, the pleasures and lessons of reading clearly play an important thematic role in *Psyché*. Bernard Beugnot has gone even further in a direction that directly concerns us here when he sees in *Psyché* "la représentation idéale de la textualité classique" ("Spécularités classiques" 180). In this chapter, I propose to expand on Collinet's insight into this aspect of La Fontaine's work by studying the functions of the internal readers and their readings in and of *Psyché* while reflecting on the nature of the text that figures these readers reading.

At the center of this rich and complex work lies a fundamental tension whose implications need to be explored. La Fontaine's *Psyché* is a framed narrative, the relation of an elegant afternoon of literary conversation. In the framing narrative, Poliphile invites three friends to visit the grounds and palace of Versailles. During their visit he will read to them his latest work, a retelling of the well-known legend of Psyché and Cupid.[1] The Psyché story, as we read it, is thus at a second level of narration. Within the framing narrative, Poliphile's voice will mediate his text so that a figure of speaking imposes itself on the written frame. What we read is Poliphile's oral performance, his reading of his novel, as well as his oral interpolations, his commentary on his work, and that of his friends. Speaking is thus foregrounded and lays some claim to precedence in the literary experience. The foregrounding of figures of speaking is conspicuous at every level of the work. It is apparent in the structure of the work itself—we are never allowed to forget the "presence," the voice of Poliphile as he reads his novel. His oral interpolations into his written text as well as his friends' interruptions frequently call attention to the essential orality of the work. Poliphile as writer and, for that matter, the unnamed narrator of the frame story affect an oralizing, "negligent" style.[2] In the central digression on literature, the literary form (dialogue) and the theoretical claims made about literature valorize the spoken work. Indeed, as Jacqueline Van Baelen (177-86) has shown, La Fontaine's aesthetics, of which *Psyché* is perhaps the clearest statement, depends on theatrical modes of presence, not the least of which is the unmediated presence of the human voice. There is, however, another dimension to this problem which Paul Zumthor makes explicit in his essay on *La Lettre et la voix*:

> Lorsque le poète ou son interprète chante ou récite (que le texte soit improvisé ou mémorisé), sa voix seule confère à celui-ci son autorité. [. . .] Si le poète ou l'interprète, en revanche, lit dans un livre ce qu'entendent ses auditeurs, l'autorité provient plutôt du livre comme tel, objet visuellement perçu au centre du spectacle performanciel; l'écriture, avec les valeurs qu'elle signifie et maintient, est explicitement partie à la performance. (19)

In *Psyché* of course, Poliphile's book, like his voice, is at a second level of narration. Nonetheless, I can conclude with Zumthor that writing, with the values that it signifies and maintains, is explicitly a part of the performance. This chapter will, within the representation of reading and speaking, attempt to locate and differentiate the part of the voice and the part of the text.

In spite of the asserted and implied orality of *Psyché*, there is an aspect to the work that cannot be seen merely as the representation of speaking. This is best seen in Poliphile's novel *Psyché*, which is in one sense a text about the interpretation of texts. At every step of the way, Psyché must confront texts that it is vitally important for her to interpret: the oracle on which her fate

Inscribing the Voice 67

depends; Cupid's palace, which could tell her story, if she knew how it should be read; the temple inscriptions in Part 2; the Myrtis and Megano story that Psyché reads on the wall of their mausoleum; and a final oracle, which, because Psyché cannot read it, precipitates the catastrophic confrontation between Psyché and her enemy, Venus. On the frame level, documents are cited as well: the mysterious manuscript that purports to explain Cupid's intransigence in remaining unseen, for example. The status of these texts cited within the space of the novel needs to be studied in relation to the feigned orality of the work. I would first like to show how readers of La Fontaine's work become aware of this fundamental tension between voice and text and the modes of presence they imply. This can be shown by examining one reader's strategy in disambiguating the narrative levels in *Psyché*.

In his germinal article on the "Functions of the Framework in La Fontaine's *Psyché*," Nathan Gross detects a dissonance in the first paragraph of Poliphile's novel:

> [. . .] car Psyché (c'est ainsi que leur jeune sœur s'appelait), Psyché, dis-je, possédait tous les appas que l'imagination peut se figurer, et ceux où l'imagination même ne peut atteindre. (*OD* 134)[3]

Gross accounts for the awkwardness of this passage by assimilating it to natural speech:

> The "dis-je" suggests that Poliphile orally interpolated the parenthesis and that he is returning to the prepared text, as if he had neglected to name the heroine in the manuscript, just as he had named neither her parents nor sisters. [. . .] The parenthesis seems to show Poliphile suddenly aware of a flaw in his text, covering it up as best he can on the spot, and then caught stylistically as it were, by his carelessness. ("Functions" 582)

Poliphile's written text is thus at the very outset flawed. It breaks a composition rule relative to the naming of characters in a narrative. If one were reading Poliphile's manuscript rather than a representation of his reading of his manuscript which includes his oral commentary, the reader might just possibly notice this flaw in composition. Readers' perception of this flaw is assured by Poliphile's correction, over-correction, one might say, of his manuscript. Correction of a flaw on one level of discourse produces an ungrammaticality (in Michael Riffaterre's sense of the word) on another level of discourse. This ungrammaticality is the sign of the imbrication of two texts in a single textual space—what might be called the oral text (the transcript of Poliphile's oral performance of his novel) and the written text (Poliphile's manuscript itself).

It is significant that this stylistically marked flaw should occur when the heroine's name is mentioned for the first time, since the narrator of the framing story uses a similar stylistic device to bestow the name "Poliphile" on the first-person narrator of the Psyché story. The narrator introduces the Academy of the four friends in terms of the literary inclinations of the group as a whole:

> Ils adoraient les ouvrages des anciens, ne refusaient point à ceux des modernes les louanges qui leur sont dues, parlaient des leurs avec modestie, et se donnaient des avis sincères lorsque quelqu'un d'eux tombait dans la maladie du siècle, et faisait un livre, ce qui arrivait rarement. Poliphile y était le plus sujet (c'est le nom que je donnerai à l'un de ces quatre amis). (*OD* 127)

The narrator's "flawed" style prefigures Poliphile's in that a character is named without preparation and this "flaw" is corrected parenthetically. This time, however, the narratorial *je* is the author of the frame story, La Fontaine, for lack of another name. It is difficult to see how this parenthetical correction could be naturalized by supposing a human voice correcting a faulty text without imagining a regression of scenes of reading in which each successive narrator would have a status in the text similar to that of Poliphile. The only fair conclusion is that this passage is written in a "negligent" style that imitates orality without representing it as such.

The narrator's parenthetical intrusion at this point calls attention to the naming of the frame characters. They are given names ("c'est le nom que je donnerai [. . .]"); they do not have names. As we observed in Chapter 2, seventeenth-century stage names are designed to be perfectly transparent to anyone with a little Greek. The names of the frame characters are appropriate proper names in that they are interpretable, transparent figures of the characters' temperaments and literary preferences.[4] But what of Psyché, the only named human in Poliphile's novel? (The god Cupid is a special case, as we shall soon see.) First of all, neither La Fontaine nor Poliphile can take responsibility for her name. It comes to us through a long textual tradition partially cited by La Fontaine in the preface and by Poliphile in his liminary verses.

But *psyché* (as a common noun) has meaning apart from the story in which Psyché is a character. *Psyché* means "soul" as much as *Poliphile* means "lover of many things." If we are meant to interpret one, why not the other? Reading *Psyché* as *Soul* in Poliphile's novel cannot help but generate an allegorical reading. A program of reading seems built into the name of the heroine. However, modern commentators are all but unanimous in proclaiming that La Fontaine's *Psyché* is not allegorical, at least not in the way Apuleius's novel and the *Hypnerotomachia Poliphili* are.[5] The Psyché legend as La Fontaine received it had already been read and reread, told and retold, who knows how many times since classical antiquity. One of La Fontaine's goals in *Psyché* was to rewrite the legend as a *texte de plaisir*, independent of past versions, to strip away the accretions of past readings that have attached themselves to the Psyché story. His irony, his *badinage*, and his self-conscious refusal to take his story too seriously are perhaps surface manifestations of his refusal to read the legend as it had always been read before. His rewriting attempts to re-invest Psyché's name with the density, opacity, uninterpretability, denied to "Poliphile," "Gélaste," "Ariste," and "Acante." Perhaps it is this very refusal to interpret the name *Psyché* that engenders on another level the thematic representation of the failure to interpret.

The representation of the failure to interpret emerges thematically from the outset of Poliphile's telling of the Psyché story. Psyché's adventure in Part 1 depends entirely on her inability to read the will of the gods written in their oracle. Here is the first and, for Psyché, most troublesome of the four stanzas that compose the oracle:

> L'époux que les Destins gardent à votre fille
> Est un monstre cruel qui déchire les cœurs,
> Qui trouble maint Etat, détruit mainte famille,
> Se nourrit de soupirs, se baigne dans les pleurs.
>
> (*OD* 138)

This oracle is the pretext for a debate between our two authors, La Fontaine writing his preface and Poliphile discussing his novel with his friends. Of course this debate is really a *dialogue de sourds*, since there is no way their communication could be staged. In the preface, La Fontaine calls this first oracle the "nœud de la fable" (*OD* 124) and spends almost a third of his preface in an elaborate justification of its style. Oracles, he says, should be both short and ambiguous. His is neither. Poliphile explains this badly written oracle by claiming that it contains the glosses of the priests. The author of the preface does not find this rationalization very convincing, since even the priests do not understand what the god makes them say. This oracle seems to me emblematic of the hermeneutic displacement inherent perhaps in all reading and writing. As Psyché receives the oracle, it is already the product of an uncontrolled series of glosses, periphrases, latent interpretations, whose practical effect for her is the regression of meaning. Psyché and her parents are naive readers who fail to grasp the rhetorical mode of all oracles, their obligatory ambiguity. For Psyché, words mean what they say. Language is, or ought to be, transparent; a word, the sign of an idea, itself the sign of a thing. The oracle said that Psyché was to marry a monster, and all the evidence to the contrary can only partially dispel that word.

Poliphile and friends are, to some extent, ironic readers. For them, the oracle is the corruption of a truth hidden below the textual surface of the oracle. For La Fontaine, a good deal of the interest lies in the space between a literal interpretation of the oracle and the sophisticated, ironic reading proposed by Poliphile. It remains to be shown how the text invites, at a third level, the ironization of Poliphile's ironic reading. For Psyché, however, the only way to undo the "nœud de la fable," to verify its falseness and thereby to reaffirm the transparence of language, is by confronting the sign and its referent, the "monster" and the husband.

This confrontation between the word of the oracle and the physical presence of her husband first takes place in the famous grotto scene, an episode La Fontaine claims as his own invention. Psyché begs her invisible husband to let her see him. He refuses: "C'est une chose qui ne se peut, pour des raisons que je ne saurais même vous dire." "Je ne saurais donc vous aimer," she replies. Her words cut deeply:

> Les paroles de l'oracle lui revenaient à l'esprit. Le moyen de les accorder avec cette douceur passionnée que son époux lui faisait paraître? Celui qui empoisonnait, qui brûlait, qui faisait ses jeux de tortures, soupirer pour un simple mot! Cela semblait tout à fait étrange à notre héroïne; et, à vrai dire, tant de tendresse en un monstre était une chose assez nouvelle. (*OD* 151)

Psyché's "Je ne saurais donc vous aimer" is in this context more than a conventional display of *dépit amoureux*. Unknown to her, her words attack the name of the god in his essence: Love. Not to love, or in this case to negate the verbal form of the god's name, is blasphemy.

Inscribing the Voice

It is at this moment when Love is at his most vulnerable that Poliphile takes up his cause. The word *monstre* echoes through the page. It has been cut from the text of the ambiguous oracle and has become in this scene Psyché's special curse and Poliphile's special joke. If Psyché is ever to be happy, this word must be exorcized. It could have been exorcized by an ironic reading of the oracle, but only by finding a new text, so to speak, for this free-floating signifier can the word lose its power to hurt Psyché and amuse Poliphile.

For Poliphile's contemporaries, there is already a sense in which Cupid is a monster. In unnecessarily inflicting pain on Psyché, he is a monster in the hyperbolic language of gallantry.[6] Poliphile's *badinage* refigurates the word along these lines while attempting to ironize at the expense of Psyché's too literal understanding of the word. These two distinct levels of meaning coincide in Poliphile's motivation of Cupid's inexplicable decision to remain unseen. Cupid's conduct is a refinement in the code of gallantry that seems, paradoxically, to block the understanding of the word in a hyperbolic, gallant sense, a sense Poliphile's *badinage* suggests to the reader. The insignificant suffering Cupid causes Psyché by not letting her see him is only inflicted to keep her love. On the frame level at least, Cupid is not a monster in any sense of the word except perhaps in the very weakest:

> [. . .] que ceux qui sont beaux se cachent, c'est un prodige dans la nature; et peut-être n'y avait-il que cela de monstrueux en la personne de notre époux. (*OD* 152)

Poliphile needs to explain away Cupid's monstrousness, and his inexplicable conduct. Poliphile's account of how he was able to remotivate Cupid's stubbornness is also La Fontaine's playful reflection on the intertextual practices of his time: "Après en avoir cherché la raison, voici ce que j'ai trouvé dans un manuscrit qui est venu depuis peu à ma connaissance" (*OD* 152). Poliphile transfers responsibility for this explanation to a "manuscript," which allows him to propose a new motivation for Cupid's incomprehensible behavior. The assumption, consonant with the classical theory of *imitatio*, is that only a pre-existent text can authenticate a new reading in a legend already well-known to writer and audience.[7] According to Poliphile, this manuscript has been stylistically incorporated into his novel so that the only sign of its presence as citation is his assertion of its presence. However, the solution the manuscript proposes to the interpretive difficulties caused by Cupid's conduct is not very satisfying. For once, Psyché, Poliphile, and reader find themselves in agreement: "Psyché se paya de ces raisons, ou, si elle ne s'en paya, elle fit semblant de s'en payer" (*OD* 154). In order for the story to progress, reader, writer, and character must accept insufficient reasons as explanations for Cupid's behavior. The superposition of the "manuscript" on the frame level fails to displace the oracle as the founding document of the Psyché legend.

***

Many commentators have shown how Part 2 of *Psyché* differs stylistically as well as thematically from Part 1. The overall style is more sustained; there are fewer interruptions and interpolations in Poliphile's reading of his text.[8] La Fontaine himself notes in his preface that four of the principal episodes in Part 2 are his own invention, not to be found in Apuleius. It is interesting that two of these episodes, the "Old Man and Shepherdesses" and "Myrtis and Megano," directly involve the problematics of reading and interpretation.

The "Old Man" episode opens with two cases of mistaken identity. Both Poliphile and Psyché commit the Quixotic fault of reading the world as if it were a book. Psyché's error is based on a naive, surface resemblance. After narrowly escaping Venus's emissaries, she sees an old man:

> Un très beau vieillard, et blanc comme un lis, mais non pas si frais, se disposait à passer. Son front était plein de rides, dont la plus jeune était presque aussi ancienne que le déluge. Aussi Psyché le prit pour Deucalion. (*OD* 195)

Of course the old man is not Deucalion. Psyché's misidentification seems oddly enough to be motivated by Poliphile's comparison, since "déluge" and Deucalion belong to the same myth, the same intertextual space. The humor of the passage is a result of the blurring of narrative levels, a reversal of intertextual cause and effect. Psyché deduces the identity of the old man by taking literally a cliché which can properly belong only to Poliphile's discourse.

In the following paragraph, there is another kind of misreading. Speaking in his own voice, Poliphile interjects a literary allusion: "Il me semble que je vois les vieillards de Troie qui se préparent à la guerre en voyant Hélène" (*OD* 195). He is, of course, alluding to a famous scene in the *Iliad*. The comparison between these two scenes is motivated by their common motif: an old man sees a beautiful woman. The point of the passage in the *Iliad* is, however, exactly the opposite, that not even Helen is worth a war and should be sent back immediately.[9] Unlike these old men, the old man in the Psyché story is willing to risk his life for her. How should this mistaken allusion be read? Gross reads it as a sign of Poliphile's lack of pedantry and as another oral interpolation into his written text ("Functions" 582). I believe it should also be read in relation to Psyché's mistake. Poliphile as author gives in to the same temptation as Psyché. He reads what is not "there." Texts—the Deucalion myth, the Psyché legend, Poliphile's manuscript, La Fontaine's representation of Poliphile's reading of his manuscript—jumble together in an intertextual confusion that requires a third-level reader to set straight. "Mistakes" on one or more levels of discourse are the signs of their mutual interference, intertextuality at play.

In the calm and relative safety of the old man's cave, Psyché once again takes up poetry as she had in Cupid's palace:

> La commodité du lieu obligea Psyché d'y faire des vers, d'en rendre les hêtres participants. Elle rappela les idées de la poésie que les Nymphes lui avaient données. Voici à peu près le sens de ses vers: (*OD* 204)

Readers are explicitly invited to compare the analogous scene in Part 1 where, for lack of a name for her absent husband, Psyché tells her troubles to the trees and the streams in the palace gardens:

> "Hélas! disait-elle aux arbres, je ne saurais graver sur votre écorce que mon nom seul, car je ne sais pas celui de la personne que j'aime." Après les arbres, elle s'adressait aux ruisseaux [. . .]. (*OD* 155)

Poliphile in this scene represents her speech as a sonnet ("Ruisseaux, enseignez-moi [. . .]" [156]) in which a very curious displacement is already apparent. Speaking in verse is substituted for writing the name of Psyché's husband. In the corresponding episode in Part 2, "en rendre les hêtres participants" is first of all interpretable as a conventional sign of literary apostrophe, analogous, it would seem, to her reciting her poem to the streams. It is also a sign of the futility of her discourse. Poliphile this time translates Psyché's lament as *stances*. Here is the final stanza:

> C'est ainsi qu'en un bois Psyché contait aux arbres
> Sa douleur, dont l'excès faisait fendre les marbres,

> Habitants de ces lieux.
> Rochers, qui l'écoutiez avec quelque tendresse,
> Souvenez-vous des pleurs qu'au fort de sa tristesse
> Ont versés ses beaux yeux.
>
> (*OD* 205)

    This final stanza, like the description of Cupid's tapestry I will examine in the next chapter, seems to confuse Poliphile's narrative voice and Psyché's *stances*. Writing in the third person and past tense, Poliphile has taken back the verse form he "gave" to Psyché in his translation of her poem. One might reasonably expect Psyché's poem to be a discrete, closed poem, the translation of Psyché's voice. If Psyché's voice here is verse, then Poliphile's ought to be prose. Poliphile as narrator has no place using "Psyché's" verse, but Poliphile calls attention to his presence as narrator, thus reclaiming "her" verse as "his" verse.

    The problematics of the case become richer when we learn that our initial interpretation of "en rendre les hêtres participants" has been inadequate. Psyché had not only spoken to the trees in verse translated by Poliphile as *stances*; she had carved her poem on their bark. What had first been taken to be a representation of her speaking must now be taken as writing in its most basic material sense as inscription. For moderns, Psyché's act of writing might recall myths of the origin of writing retained in the etymologies of Western languages (Latin *liber* = "book" and "bark"; German *Buch* = "book" and "beech tree" [Zumthor, *Langue* 13-19]), while La Fontaine's contemporaries certainly noticed one of pastoral literature's most enduring motifs.[10]

    Where there is writing there must also be reading, and, in fact, Psyché does have a reader, the younger of the two shepherdesses, who has been forbidden to read novels. For Poliphile, novels have an educational value:

> Il est de l'amour comme du jeu; c'est prudemment fait que d'en apprendre toutes les ruses, non pas pour les pratiquer, mais afin de s'en garantir. Si jamais vous avez des filles, laissez-les lire. (*OD* 206)

The shepherdess defends her right to read by denying the closure even of her world to the unexpected appearance of people and of texts:

> Psyché n'a pas d'ailes, ni nous non plus; nous nous rencontrons cependant. Mais, à propos de Psyché, que signifient les paroles qu'elle a gravées sur nos hêtres? (*OD* 206)

Even if Psyché did not tell her story to the shepherdesses, her poem is there, carved on the beech trees. Texts permeate the world, and for that reason alone it is foolish to forbid reading.

This intertextual movement on the story level is mirrored on the frame level as well. The "Old Man and Shepherdesses" episode is defined only by Psyché's passing through. Readers never hear the end of their story. As a novel within a novel, it is left open, incomplete. Poliphile justifies not finishing this episode by invoking the limits he has set for himself, his *unité d'action*:

> La famille du vieillard arriva heureusement dans le lieu où elle avait dessein de s'établir. Je vous conterais ses aventures si je ne m'étais point prescrit des bornes plus resserrées. Peut-être qu'un jour les mémoires que j'ai recueillis tomberont entre les mains de quelqu'un qui s'exercera sur cette matière, et qui s'en acquittera mieux que moi: maintenant je n'achèverai que l'histoire de notre héroïne. (*OD* 212)

The end of the "Old Man" episode is here represented as a collection of already written fragments, "mémoires," collected by the author but refused access to *Psyché* because they are inessential to the main story line. These fragments are ironically placed in the public domain, at the disposal of anyone willing to work on them, as Poliphile has worked on Apuleius's story. The intertextual movement illustrated here on both the story level and on the frame level is the inverse of the movement in Part 1, in which a fictive manuscript was assimilated to Poliphile's novel for the purpose of explaining Cupid's inexplicable conduct. In both cases, the coming and going of texts in the author's commentary on his work mirrors the coming and going of characters on the story level. The textual space of the Psyché story remains open to the intersection of other texts, and closure (of the whole novel, of an episode) invariably results in a textual residue ("mémoires," "manuscrits").

***

The "Myrtis and Megano" episode is one of the more telling examples of the problematics of reading in *Psyché*. On the story level, it represents another digression on Psyché's way to her enemy, Venus. Poliphile first tells the story of Myrtis and Megano in his own voice. His telling of the story is motivated by his desire to explain the origins of the adjacent temple, where Psyché will finally confront Venus:

> Sur le point du jour, elle [Psyché] arriva à un lieu nommé: les deux sépultures. Je vous en dirai la raison, parce que l'origine du temple en dépend. (*OD* 223-24)

Myrtis and Megano were two beautiful women chosen for King Philocharès. Megano, although perhaps the more beautiful of the two, lacked a certain charm, Myrtis's strong point. For that reason, Myrtis alone, renamed Aphrodisée, found favor with the king. Megano, now called Anaphrodite, died of the disgrace. Myrtis Aphrodisée lived long and happily with the king and, in her testament, asked to be buried near Megano. After her death Philocharès had their tombs built in accordance with Myrtis's wishes.

Poliphile ends the story of Myrtis and Megano with an account of how the tombs came to be built and, in a barely noticeable transition, with a physical description of the two tombs. The description includes a quotation of the epitaphs, which also tell the story of Myrtis and Megano, this time in the first person. The epitaphs, rather than completing Poliphile's telling of the story, double it, and almost replace it, since we seem to have arrived at the source, the authentic words of Myrtis and Megano engraved on stone. Here, for example, is Myrtis's side of the story engraved on her side of the tomb:

> Vous qui allez visiter ce temple, arrêtez un peu et écoutez-moi. De simple bergère que j'étais née, je me suis vue reine. Ce qui m'a procuré ce bien, ce n'est pas tant la beauté que ce sont les grâces. J'ai plu et cela suffit. C'est ce que j'avais à vous dire. Honorez ma tombe de quelques fleurs; et pour récompense, veuille la déesse des Grâces que vous plaisiez! (*OD* 225)

In accordance with the rules of the epitaph genre, the long-dead Myrtis and Megano are made to speak in their own voices to a fictive passerby. They tell their story, request a memorial offering, and so on. Within this highly formalized genre, readers may well be struck especially by Megano's stylistic liberties. Her voice attempts to break through in a conversational tone, a "negligent" style, that seems to guarantee the authenticity of the quotation by assimilating it to the spoken language: "mais je n'étais pas, dit-on, assez jolie. Cela se peut-il? Oui, cela se peut" (*OD* 225). This tone is all the more surprising, since in framing the episode, Poliphile has already told us that Megano's epitaph is not in fact her own final testament. The tomb inscription, like Psyché's poem written on the beech trees, is another figure of absence. The

Inscribing the Voice

words inscribed on her tomb were never spoken by her. It was Philocharès who had the tombs built, not Megano, nor even Myrtis, who died before they could be built. Unlike the tombs of Myrtis and Megano, the neighboring Temple of Venus is signed:

> A l'entour de la médaille à deux têtes: c'étaient celles des fondateurs, on voyait écrit: *Philocharès et Myrtis Aphrodisée, son épouse, ont dédié ce temple à Venus*. Sur chaque base des deux colonnes les plus proches de la porte, étaient entaillés ces mots: *Ouvrage de Lysimante*, nom de l'architecte apparemment. (*OD* 226)

Perhaps Philocharès had the epitaphs written on the tombs by the architect at Myrtis's request to make Myrtis's glory the greater by contrast to the unhappy Megano. Texts as they are cited in *Psyché* always seem to beg the ghostly question: Who is speaking here? A style, a tone, that seems most authentic, closest to the voice of Megano herself, is revealed as writing whose author (Megano? Myrtis in her testament? Philocharès? the architect?) is lost in the intertext.[11]

What is true for the origin, the original inscription, of the epitaphs, is also true for their reading. The sentences that frame the quotation of the temple inscriptions are all in the passive voice: "ces mots se lisaient," "ces autres paroles étaient [. . .]," "ces autres paroles se rencontraient." These passives seem to imply the immutability of the text carved on stone for the ages. Then, without transition in the description of the tombs, Psyché reappears. Our tour of the tomb has also been her tour of the tomb. She has just read what we have just read, and Poliphile's quotation of the tomb inscriptions is now seen as motivated by Psyché's reading. Readers at once recognize here an important lesson for Psyché. Psyché herself does not.

In two of the four episodes in Part 2 of *Psyché* that La Fontaine claims as his own invention, public inscriptions, their writing, and their interpretation play an important role. This is not entirely surprising in a period that has been accurately characterized as "l'âge de l'inscription" (Vuilleumier 291). However, inscriptions, probably because they are not properly literary and do not belong wholly to the plastic arts, have received less critical attention than they merit.[12] Inscriptions are, however, particularly interesting for the theory of the text in that in inscriptions, writing is most itself, most distanced from the voice. As we have seen, the problematics of the relation of voice to epitaph, of orality to textuality, emerge clearly in the "Myrtis and Megano" episode of

Psyché. Within inscriptions the materiality of writing thus becomes a critical problem. The inscription integrates two signifying media, monument and text, within a single geometry. The result is, as in the emblem, a unity of greater signifying potential than either alone. The monument itself is not an indifferent support for the text. It is often assumed that words have exactly the same meaning on whatever material they are inscribed; the material support ought to be an indifferent matrix. In *Psyché*, however, the manner and mode of inscription is significant. It matters whether the text is engraved on tombs, as in the "Myrtis and Megano" episode, or on beech trees, as in the "Old Man" episode.

These two episodes in *Psyché* are not the only works in which La Fontaine has shown his interest in inscriptions. In the curious double fable "Le Loup, la Chèvre et le Chevreau"—"Le Loup, la Mère et l'Enfant" (*Fables* 4.15-16), the moral of the fable and its writing, its inscription, is represented within the fable in a way that relates the inscription and the emblem. At the end of the second fable, the peasants cut off the paw and the head of the unfortunate wolf:

> Le Seigneur du Village à sa porte les mit,
> Et ce dicton picard à l'entour fut écrit:
> *Biaux chires Leups, n' écoutez mie*
> *Mère tenchent chen fieux qui crie.*

This "peasant" emblem shares the same structure as more noble examples that still grace classical monuments. In the seventeenth century, one of the major questions facing authors of inscriptions was in which language inscriptions on public monuments should be written (Vuilleumier). Should inscriptions be in Latin, the language of the letter par excellence, or in French, the maternal language, the language of the voice? In this fable, the inscription in *picard* curiously conflates the tendencies of the two languages. For La Fontaine's educated readers, *picard* no doubt connotes orality, while its "foreignness" renders it difficult, almost unreadable. It is a text that needs to be deciphered.

In a fable much closer in spirit to the *Psyché* episodes, "Le Vieillard et les Trois Jeunes Hommes" (*Fables* 11.8), the fable itself is figured as an inscription. Three young men, one at a time, mock an old man's optimism:

> Un Octogénaire plantait.
> Passe encore de bâtir, mais planter à cet âge!

Inscribing the Voice

The old man, of course, lives to bury the young men:

> Et pleurés du Vieillard, il grava sur leur marbre
> Ce que je viens de raconter.

Epitaph and fable are in these closing verses of the fable perfectly coincident.[13] Once again, La Fontaine stages within a fictional work instances of reading and writing that reveal the pragmatics of textuality in the classical period.

***

As one might expect in a classical text, *Psyché*, on the surface at least, betrays the fundamental prejudice for speech and against writing that Jacques Derrida has found underlying all Western metaphysics. Indeed, *Psyché* allegorizes the search for full presence (of Cupid, of Love), a presence constantly deferred through the writing of the fiction that represents it. However, the device of multiple levels of narration, the representation of the novel as the oral performance of a text, the citation of unassimilated or partially unassimilated texts on both levels of narration and their inevitable interference, invite within *Psyché* the replication of scenes of reading and writing so that within a framed narrative seemingly given over to the modulations of voice, writing and reading necessarily impose themselves as theme.

6
Description, Representation, and Interpretation

Les Amours de Psyché et de Cupidon

Western culture probably can never give up elaborating the web of relations it ceaselessly traces between the visual and the verbal. Our critical discourses about language and vision are so fundamentally intertwined in their metaphoricity that writing outside of them is no doubt impossible.[1] While the modern tendency, at least since Lessing, has been to treat this figural interpenetration as essentially problematic, the French seventeenth century found itself in somewhat easy possession of a theory of production and a practice of reading inherited from the Italian Renaissance that seemed to relate these two modes of sign production in an elegant and satisfying way. Painting was the visualization of a text, and what we have come to call literature involved "seeing" portraits, tableaus, landscapes, or even works of visual art. Horace's often misread dictum that poetry should be like a picture (*ut pictura poesis*) became the point of departure and the inevitable conclusion of most critical discourse on art and literature in the classical period.[2] At the same time, readers tended to evaluate literary description in terms of the text's capacity to summon images.

As we have seen in the previous chapter, *Psyché* is an excellent laboratory for examining readerly stategies available for the interpretation of written texts in the seventeenth century; but written texts are not the only sign systems available to Psyché or to Poliphile. In this chapter, I would like to continue my reading of *Psyché* in order to consider another aspect of this diffuse, disconcerting, and at times difficult text, that is, the description of works of art, statuary, tapestries, paintings, and monuments, and the representation of their interpretation or, more precisely, the representation of the failure to interpret them in the framing narrative and in the Psyché story.

Psyché as novel is not only a tale, the narration of events; it contains long descriptions in prose and in verse in which works of visual art play an extremely important role.[3] The framing narrative includes extended descriptions in prose and in verse of the marvels of Versailles. Certain aspects of the framing narrative are reflected in the Psyché tale itself, an important part of which takes place in Cupid's palace, described as the sum of all that was beautiful in art, architecture, and literature. Here, for example, is how Poliphile evokes Cupid's palace:

> Je vous en ferais la description si j'étais plus savant dans l'architecture que je ne suis. A ce défaut, vous aurez recours au palais d'Apollidon, ou bien à celui d'Armide; ce m'est tout un. Quant aux jardins, voyez ceux de Falerine: ils vous pourront donner quelque idée des lieux que j'ai à décrire.
>
> > Assemblez, sans aller si loin,
> > Vaux, Liancourt, et leur naïades,
> > Y joignant, en cas de besoin,
> > Ruel avecque ses cascades [. . .].
>
> (*OD* 148-49)

Cupid's palace is for Poliphile a compilation of fictive palaces (the palaces of Apollidon and of Armide) and of palaces that in principle could be known by visiting them (Vaux, Liancourt, Ruel [that is, Rueil]).

As we have seen in the previous chapter, Versailles contains the Psyché story as the scene of Poliphile's performance of his novel. He reads Part 1 at the Grotto of Tethys, which contains visual representations of tritons, nymphs, and graces, all characters or potential characters in his novel.[4] It is this aspect of the relation between Versailles and Cupid's palace that Nathan Gross calls "mythological realism" ("Functions" 580). Readers are somehow more prepared to accept Psyché's fictive world because Versailles exists. Psyché's story is then a sort of animated Versailles.[5] La Fontaine suggests this possibility, consonant with the *ut pictura poesis* representational model, in a sustained description of the grotto statuary (132 verses). A parenthetical intervention in which the narrator excuses himself for exceeding the mimetic bounds of description is particularly telling in this respect. He makes one of Apollo's serving girls blush:

> Elle rougit parfois, parfois baisse la vue,
> (Rougit, autant que peut rougir une statue:

> Ce sont des mouvements qu'au défaut du sculpteur
> Je veux faire passer dans l'esprit du lecteur.)
>
> *(OD* 132)

The author of the descriptive verse, who is also the reader of the statuary group, is doing no more than what readers are expected to do, namely to expand and complete the mimesis. In the description of a work of art, it is acceptable to make a statue blush, since a statue is a representation of a character who could and, in the situation described, probably would blush. The implication is that these "mouvements" are justifiable in descriptive poetry because verse and statue are ultimately representations of the same narrative content. The reader must assign description that exceeds referential *vraisemblance* to this pre-existing content plane. Versailles as frame thus potentially includes the Psyché story. Her story could be (but is not) a sculptural group, animated "au défaut du sculpteur" by the poet. Versailles actually includes the Psyché story only as the scene of Poliphile's reading. Her "presence" in Versailles is not grounded in a visual representation, but through Poliphile's words "present" on the day he read his novel to his friends. This play of multiple inclusions and multiple modes of presence is particularly conspicuous in the descriptions of Cupid's palace. Cupid's palace includes Versailles in that Cupid's palace is a sort of architectural encyclopedia and universal anthology of all love stories. For Psyché, who will come to Cupid's palace to learn about love, it is the ideal university, since it contains:

> [. . .] tout ce qui est contenu sur ce point dans les archives de l'Univers, soit pour le passé, soit pour l'avenir, à l'exception de son aventure, qu'on lui cacha, quelque prière qu'elle fît aux Nymphes de la lui apprendre. *(OD* 155)

A similar passage, several pages before, stresses this same aspect of Cupid's palace "[. . .] où, par un enchantement prophétique, ce qui n'était pas encore et ce qui ne devait jamais être se rencontrait" *(OD* 145).[6] Cupid's palace thus claims logical and historical priority, and Versailles becomes in some senses a quotation of Cupid's palace. The statues, for example, that decorate Cupid's palace are emblematic not of a finite set of stories drawn from classical mythology, but of the whole text, of all that has been done or written on the subject of love. As text it is absolutely centered. There is a transcendent signified that makes sense of the whole. Reading the palace, however, is possible only if readers can abstract a common property (love) from the infinite, multiform representations that make up the palace. For Psyché, this palace of representation can be maintained only at the price of her renunciation of the visual presence of her husband. The moment the abstraction, the common property, becomes proper, in other words when Psyché sees Cupid and can name him, the palace ceases to exist. In this sense, Psyché's preoccupation with seeing her husband is analogous to her inability to name him. Literature is born in the space of this absence in Psyché's apostrophe to the trees, the prelude to her sonnet that we examined in the previous chapter.

Given certain assumptions about the nature and function of the representation of the visual in the seventeenth century, some of the descriptions of Cupid's palace are very strange indeed. Even the marvelous does not escape the constraints of a given culture's representational system. The marvelous merely serves to emphasize them by playing with them. While it is certainly true, as Michael Riffaterre has observed in his essay on the semiotics of description in seventeenth-century poetry, that the properly literary function of description may not even be to describe, it is nonetheless true that readers expect to naturalize referentially what purports to be a description, and especially a description of a work of visual art.[7] The literary description of a work of visual art, or *ekphrasis*, functions precisely by limiting readers' recourse to other modes of interpretation exclusively in favor of visualization.[8] Thus a description of a work of art, whether real or fictive, that disrupts the expected strategies of naturalization through visualization had better be able to recuperate the anomaly on another level of significance.

For the purposes of this chapter, I would now like to consider two examples from *Psyché* that stand out as exemplary of the thematic representation of the failure to interpret visual documents. The first is from the framing narrative set at Versailles and the second, and more telling, from the Psyché story itself. Both involve an internal reader's response to a tapestry, and both episodes are structured so that, among the correspondences, resonances, and analogies that articulate frame and tale, these two moments are easily seen to allude to each other.

Early in the frame narrative, the four friends visit the interior of Louis's palace. The narrator passes over most of the details, since, as he says, a detailed description would simply take too much time. Our attention, and that of the four friends, is drawn, however, to one marginal, seemingly insignificant detail located nonetheless at the signifying center of Versailles, the king's bedchamber:

Description, Representation, and Interpretation 85

Entre autres beautés, ils s'arrêtèrent longtemps à considérer le lit, la tapisserie et les sièges dont on a meublé la chambre et le cabinet du Roi. C'est un tissu de la Chine, plein de figures qui contiennent toute la religion de ce pays-là. Faute de brachmane, nos quatre amis n'y comprirent rien. (*OD* 130)

The narrator passes over what would seem the essential, the fact that Versailles as a signifying system is centered exactly here, that the king's empty bed alludes to the absent king, and concentrates instead on a seemingly frivolous detail that makes no sense to the four friends. The tapestry that covers every available surface in the king's bedchamber is a visual document purported to have a certain significance, while its central place is a possible indicator of its potential importance in a palace where everything is held to mean something. The assertion that it contains the "whole religion" ("toute la religion de ce pays-là") might even indicate that its interpretation might be of some importance. In fact, "ce pays-là" in this context becomes slightly ambiguous. It of course refers to China, an hyperbole of the incomprehensible to the seventeenth-century mentality, but perhaps "ce pays-là" includes Versailles as well. What is lacking in this scene of reading, or rather nonreading, is a competent interpreter, a "Brahmin," who can decipher the impenetrable code in which the tapestry is written. The four friends must dismiss the signifying potential of the tapestry and reduce it to its merely decorative function. As readers they are in much the same position in Louis's palace as Psyché will soon be in Cupid's. Meaning or the presumption of meaning is everywhere, and to fail to recognize this fact, or to recognize it and be unable to decipher the message, can have untoward consequences. One example will suffice to suggest the implications of the failure to interpret within the framing narrative.

After their tour of the palace, the four friends settle down in the Grotto of Tethys to hear Poliphile's tale. This grotto is a cavernous imitation of an elegant salon in which the lamps spray water instead of light. Two favorite baroque antitheses are thus resolved in this witty construction; artifice and nature, fire and water, exchange roles. The narrator of the frame story is expansive in his praise of this exceptional site, but notes a tiny element of danger:

> Mille jets, dont la pluie à l'entour se partage,
> Mouillent également l'imprudent et le sage.
>
> (*OD* 133)

The four friends are competent readers who recognize the substitution of water for light and its potential danger, which they agree to leave to the unsophisticated:

> Les quatre amis ne voulurent point être mouillés; ils prièrent celui qui leur faisait voir la grotte de réserver ce plaisir pour le bourgeois ou pour l'Allemand [. . .]. (*OD* 133)

What other traps await the unwary or incompetent reader? In the Psyché story itself, the absolute necessity, and the impossibility, of interpreting written texts and visual documents is explicitly thematized. The monitory aspect of the Psyché story may have been lost on the four tourists in Louis's palace; it should not be lost on readers who in their reading retrace simultaneously both itineraries.

Early in Poliphile's reading of the Psyché tale, Psyché finds herself in that marvelous palace I alluded to earlier that can only be described as an anthology of all palaces, real and imagined. It is the palace of Psyché's unseen husband, who is, according to the oracle that founded her destiny, a "monster" (*OD* 138). In spite of what La Fontaine says in his preface to *Psyché* about his treatment of the oracle (*OD* 124-25), this oracle is just as ambiguous as it ought to be. It is perfectly clear to all, except Psyché and family, that her unseen husband is Cupid, Love itself. The nymphs, her guides and attendants, repeat this message in an attempt to reveal to her the meaning of the palace she is in:

> Sans cet Amour, tant d'objets ravissants,
> Lambris dorés, bois, jardins, et fontaines,
> N'ont point d'appas qui ne soient languissants,
> Et leurs plaisirs sont moins doux que ses peines.
> Des jeunes cœurs c'est le suprême bien:
> Aimez, aimez; tout le reste n'est rien.
>
> (*OD* 143)

Psyché still does not understand. Like the four friends at Versailles, she is taken on a guided tour of the palace, which encodes the same message in a variety of visual texts. Poliphile as narrator of the Psyché story abridges his inventory of the interior of Cupid's palace for the same reasons that motivated the narrator of the frame story:

> Si j'entreprenais de décrire seulement la quatrième partie de ces merveilles, je me rendrais sans doute importun; car à la fin on s'ennuie de tout, et des belles choses comme du reste. (*OD* 146)

Description, Representation, and Interpretation 87

He does, however, make Psyché stop before a series of six tapestries:

> Je me contenterai donc de parler d'une tapisserie relevée d'or laquelle on fit remarquer principalement à Psyché, non tant pour l'ouvrage, quoi qu'il fût rare, que pour le sujet. (*OD* 146)

Unlike the four friends in Louis's palace, Psyché is shown this tapestry, among all the other beautiful things in the palace, because of the importance of its message rather than for its fine workmanship or its function as pure decoration. The emphasis, however, on the medium (tapestry) and on the expressed desire of the narrator to call attention to this particular element among many others equally deserving for one reason or another does serve to recall the analogous episode in the framing narrative. The subject of the tapestry should be of interest, since it is in part a visual variant of the oracle that dictated that Psyché was to marry a "monster." Psyché is herself at this point incapable of deciphering the tapestry. As a visual variant of a text already in some senses read and therefore readable to Poliphile and friends, the message of the tapestry is, however, unmistakable.

Contrary to the normal state of affairs at Cupid's palace in which Cupid-Love is everywhere signified but personally invisible, Cupid is represented, according to well-established iconological convention, as a child. Since Psyché could not know the code the tapestry is written in, it is not surprising that she cannot recognize the child for the husband. "Husband," "monster," and "child" are for her incompatible attributes. Since Psyché has never seen her husband, Cupid's various portraits fail the referential test as well; there is in this case no way to check the represented against the real. For Psyché, Cupid's "portraits" neither refer to him nor resemble him. In Psyché's case, the tapestry is exceptional in just the opposite way within the iconographical program of the palace:

> Parmi cette diversité d'objets, rien ne plut tant à la belle que de rencontrer partout son portrait, ou bien statue, ou quelque autre ouvrage de cette nature. Il semblait que ce palais fût un temple, et Psyché la déesse à qui il était consacré. (*OD* 147-48)

Psyché's portrait is everywhere except in the tapestry. For competent readers like Poliphile and friends, it is clear that the woman before whom Cupid kneels in adoration in the last panel is Psyché herself, even though her face is turned away. By inverting the normal conditions of seeing and not seeing in Cupid's palace, the tapestry raises questions for us about the representation of absence in a visual document. The problem becomes even knottier when the very impossibility of representing pictorially a signified absence must be transposed into a linguistic medium for which verbal "presence" is the logical precondition for subsequent negation.

This tapestry is an extraordinary document that purportedly translates a visual document that Psyché sees into a verbal text that Poliphile reads to his friends. While its meaning is obscure to Psyché for the reasons we have already examined, the four friends find in it merely one more retelling of all Psyché seeks to know. Our reading of this extraordinary *ekphrasis* cannot, however, be as ironically superior as Poliphile's nor as simple as Psyché's naive incomprehension. Cupid's palace is a palace of mirrors whose multiple reflections between representations of the verbal and representations of the pictorial distort the discourse through which the narrator transposes a supposedly visual, visualizable, document into a verbal description. Here, for example, are the first two stanzas in the verse description of the first tapestry in the series:

> Dans la première on voyait un chaos,
> Masse confuse, et de qui l'assemblage
> Faisait lutter contre l'orgueil des flots
> Des tourbillons d'une flamme volage.
>
> Non loin de là, dans un même monceau,
> L'air gémissait sous le poids de la terre:
> Ainsi le feu, l'air, la terre, avec l'eau,
> Entretenait une cruelle guerre.
>
> (*OD* 146-47)

We must assume that the tapestry is being described in such a way that what the tapestry signifies is the same as what these descriptive verses signify, since its meaning is the reason Psyché is shown the tapestry in the first place. We know, too, the principles of transposition from one signifying medium to another. They were amply illustrated in the first narrator's description of the grounds and palace of Versailles. Contrary to what one might at first suspect, the classical *ut pictura poesis* representational model easily admits representations that exceed the mimetic capacities of a particular medium. We have examined the case of the blushing statue. There are other

Description, Representation, and Interpretation

examples as well. In the narrator's description of a group of statues in the Grotto of Tethys, for example, we find Tritons who "[. . .] semblent panteler du chemin qu'ils ont fait." We even hear music: "Les accords de la flûte inspirent de l'amour" (*OD* 132).[9] However, the verses that purportedly describe the tapestry Psyché is seeing do seem to me problematic, since they are not simply in excess of the mimetic capacities of the visual medium. The nature of what is supposedly described is left deliberately ambiguous. The verse is a reading of the tapestry, but a reading that refuses any coherent reconstruction of the visual "original."

The first stanza evokes formlessness while insisting on the visual point of view of an observer ("on voyait"). The second, as in most ekphrastic literature, draws limits, assuring readers of the spatial integrity of the tapestry as work of art ("non loin de là," "dans un même monceau"). It also seems to be a thematic variation of the first stanza expanded along the paradigmatic axis to include all four elements at war. These two stanzas do not allow readers to naturalize the presumed pictorial content by reference to a visual model; or rather, two equally possible visual models are evoked. To complete the mimesis, should readers picture the visual representation of formlessness or allegorical renderings of the personified elements at war? These verses which purport to be a description of a picture are unrecuperable as a picture.

The third stanza seems at first to provide a key:

> Que fait l'Amour? volant de bout en bout,
> Ce jeune enfant, sans beaucoup de mystère,
> En badinant vous débrouille le tout,
> Mille fois mieux qu'un sage n'eût su faire.
>
> (*OD* 147)

If "Love" is pictured as a child, readers might be tempted to read the description of the tapestry as an allegory in which "Love" is merely represented iconographically. His function, however, seems as much interpretive as pictorial. The third verse plays on the double sense of *débrouiller*, which here means literally "to unscramble the chaos," and figuratively "to make sense of the whole." *Badiner* is in this respect ambiguous as well, since the word is used for both physical and verbal joking. Despite the assertion that Love solves the mystery, the text leaves unspecified how either of these senses is to be realized within a supposedly visual medium. The explicit comparison with a "sage" in the fourth verse perhaps emphasizes the hermeneutic function of

Love at the expense of the visual. For readers of these verses, the verbal presence of Love is sufficient to make some sense of the passage by guaranteeing the remotivation of "orgueil" and "flamme volage" in the first stanza as clichés of seventeenth-century galant language, if the reader is not too persistent in expecting Love to be both "in" the picture as a young child and "outside" the picture as the sense and sense-giver of the whole tapestry-poem.

There is at least one apparent parallel to the Versailles tapestry in these verses. In that case, the asserted or presumed sense of Louis's Chinese tapestry was irretrievable for lack of a "Brahmin," a sage who could read the language of the tapestry. In Cupid's tapestry, the "Brahmin," the only competent reader-interpreter of the ambiguous tapestry, is again Cupid-Love himself, located paradoxically within the picture in a way that defies naturalization as a picture. These verses play on the unique status of "Love" as a god capable of being represented in human proportions ("ce jeune enfant"), as a human passion which might create a community of competent lovers-interpreters (if one loved enough, one would understand these verses, or this tapestry), and finally as the transcendental signified of all representations within the palace. It is no wonder Psyché is confused.

La Fontaine's *Psyché* thus seems to be in many respects a critique of reading and, especially in the passages which deal with Versailles and Cupid's palace, a critique of interpreting works of art supposedly transposed into verbal texts. Read in this way, *Psyché* can be seen to disrupt, if ever so playfully, the *ut pictura poesis* representational model on which it is built, and might lead us to suspect that the critical articulations between eye and ear, description and its reference, were not quite so naively understood in practice as they often seem in theory. In the next chapter, I will take up just this problem in La Fontaine's tale "Le Tableau."

7
Reading (through) the Veil

"Le Tableau"

La Fontaine should have the first and last word on one of the critical problems I examined in the previous chapter:

> Les mots et les couleurs ne sont choses pareilles;
> Ni les yeux ne sont les oreilles.
>
> ("Le Tableau")

Given La Fontaine's interest in the way the verbal and the visual are related to each other, one should not perhaps be too surprised to find in his work a statement on their relationship, a statement quoted in many serious considerations on the relations between art and literature from the eighteenth century to the present.[1] It is, however, somewhat surprising to find this prestigious statement in one of La Fontaine's most licentious verse tales, "Le Tableau" (*Nouveaux contes*, 1674).[2] While it is flattering for La Fontaine's admirers to see his insight at the root of an important movement in aesthetics, the tale clearly makes few claims for itself either as theory or as "literature," belonging as it does to a popular but critically negligible genre in the classical hierarchy of genres. It does, however, seem of some interest to see how the asserted representational identity of picture and tale becomes asserted difference within the space of a single text that self-consciously displays the author's attempt to tell a very improper tale whose purported source is a painting, and how this insight is related to the pornographic verse tale in which it appears.[3] This chapter thus continues the previous one in attempting to re-enact within the text of "Le Tableau" some of the inner workings of the *ut pictura poesis* representational system.[4]

There is another aspect to "Le Tableau" that I would like to explore in this chapter. In seeking to represent decorously, as through a veil, a painting showing an explicit love scene between two nuns and a peasant boy, La Fontaine's "Le Tableau" explicitly displays the mechanism of putting sexuality into discourse. This tale thus marks a point on the line Michel Foucault has identified running from post-Tridentine reforms of the sacrament of confession to modern confessional literature:

> The Christian pastoral prescribed as a fundamental duty the task of passing everything having to do with sex through the endless mill of speech. The forbidding of certain words, the decency of expressions, all the censorings of vocabulary, might well have been only secondary devices compared to that great subjugation: ways of rendering it morally acceptable and technically useful. One could plot a line going straight from the seventeenth-century pastoral to what became its projection in literature, "scandalous" literature at that. (*Sexuality* 21)

I will be arguing that it is not indifferent at this early moment in the constitution of modern discourse that the critical articulation of the verbal and the visual should be deconstructed in a tale treating decorously the explicit representation of human sexuality. What is the reader to make of a text that attempts to identify explicitly its logic and meaning by asserting its fundamental relation to a painting within a scene of reading and viewing that negates the pictorial and thematizes that negation in the figure of the veil?

***

La Fontaine's *Nouveaux contes* appeared in 1674, coincidentally the same year as Boileau's *Art poétique*, the monumental definition of classical literary theory. Unlike La Fontaine's three preceding collections of verse tales, they were not published in Paris with Claude Barbin, his regular publisher and the society publisher par excellence in Louis XIV's reign. Instead (according to the title page), they were published in Mons, without royal *privilège*.[5] The results of this literary bravado are well known. The following year, La Reynie, lieutenant general of police, ordered the seizure of the first edition *in octavo* and two new editions (1675) *in duodecimo* because the author failed to secure permission from the royal censors and because the work contained "termes indiscrets et malhonnêtes, et dont la lecture ne peut avoir aucun effet que celui de corrompre les bonnes mœurs et d'inspirer le libertinage" (Montgrédien 118). One can only speculate on the relative importance of these two accusations, or on La Fontaine's motives in his decision not to seek a *privilège*, or even on the reasons that this official condemnation caused so few difficulties for the poet's career (Brunot 4: 296). In any case, these extra-literary considerations show that the *Nouveaux contes* were perceived as somehow different or marginal both by the author and by the authorities, and that a conscious attempt was made to bring them into the unofficial, or clandestine, book trade.[6] The *Nouveaux contes*, for literary, commercial, or ideological reasons, were marginalized deliberately, and this marginalization was perceived as significant in the seventeenth century.

***

"Le Tableau" is the only one of La Fontaine's tales to owe its inspiration to Pietro Aretino's *Ragionamenti* (1538), reputedly the most licentious of the Renaissance tale anthologies. As its name (*Dialogues*) indicates, this volume belongs to the Renaissance tradition of framed tale-telling in which characters tell stories to each other. In the first part of the *Ragionamenti*, Nanna, the principal narrator, tells Antonia the story of her youth in a convent and her initiation into the mysteries of love. Part of the young nun's training involves studying a series of frescoes, the second of which tells the story of Masetto da Lamporecchio from Boccaccio's *Decameron* (Third Day, First Story), which La Fontaine had already imitated in his second collection of tales ("Mazet de Lamporechio" [*Contes* 2.16]). The tale retold in "Le Tableau" is an incident occurring later on in the *Ragionamenti*, which Nanna observes but does not participate in, but the two examples, one studied in a painting, the other observed *in vivo*, are both key lessons in Nanna's perverse education.[7] The two stories, of course, have structural and thematic similarities in the *Ragionamenti* that La Fontaine utilizes. "Le Tableau" specifically alludes to "Mazet"; the rustic substitute for the elegant bachelor is called "a mazet," as one might say "a tartuffe." Later on, "Mazet" names a function ("son office de Mazet") rather than a character. Of course, the convent as a school for illicit love is a common theme in all three tales (F. S. Howard 18-21).

La Fontaine's decision to represent the tale of the two nuns and their lover as a painting is not directly derived from Aretino's story, but may be intertextually related through a third term, the story of Masetto represented as a painting in the *Ragionamenti*. One might explain the author's strategy as a displacement of "Mazet" and the substitution of the nun's story as "painting," while the antonomasia and other internal allusions to "Mazet" point up the suppression. This intertextual metalepsis is authorized by Aretino's text itself, which has already rendered Boccaccio's "Masetto" as a fresco. La Fontaine in a sense does to Aretino's story what Aretino had already done to Boccaccio's story. To the reader of the *Contes,* this movement in the production of the text through imitation appears as the elaboration of a temporal dimension within the *Contes.* "Mazet," the already written, is logically and somehow temporally prior to "Le Tableau," the last tale in the last of La Fontaine's tale anthologies. The Renaissance doctrine of *ut pictura poesis* taken to the letter authorizes this movement from story as recounted narrative (Boccaccio) to story as picture (Aretino), but does not satisfactorily explain why this tale should be represented as the imitation of a fictive painting.

The verse tale as invented by La Fontaine in four collections follows a general line of development that tends toward the independence of the genre from framed tale anthologies, of which Boccaccio's *Decameron* is the type par excellence and La Fontaine's most frequent source for his tales. La Fontaine's intention seems to have been to make each tale stand on its own, independent of a framing narrative or secondary fiction that in the *Decameron* and other framed tale anthologies determines the *raison d'être,* order, and theme of the tales proper. La Fontaine's tales, unlike *Psyché,* do not account for themselves as the motivated discourse of characters within a framing fiction and, therefore, are not grounded in represented speech. They claim to be no more, nor less, than text, but this rupture of tale from frame in the rewriting of the tales is felt to be a fragmentation of an "original" whole that, it seems, needs to be accounted for textually.

When La Fontaine's tales are studied in the order of their publication, one notices a trend in the four collections of tales. The authorial prologue that grounds each tale individually as the written discourse of an author (Collinet, "La Matière et l'art du prologue") recuperates loss of grounding in represented speech, in the "presence" of characters who tell their tales to each other. As we have seen, La Fontaine's own *Les Amours de Psyché et de Cupidon* represents an interesting and original compromise between what I have called in Chapter 5 the oralizing and the textualizing tendencies.

Even though La Fontaine has abandoned a framing narrative as the organizing principle of his tale anthologies, the authorial prologues mime a temporal ordering that is strictly *vraisemblable* only in an oralizing frame narrative. This is particularly apparent if one follows the nuns' theme in the

Nouveaux contes, a theme that recurs with mathematical regularity at every sixth tale, beginning with "L'Abbesse" (4.2). "Le Psautier" (4.7), "Les Lunettes" (4.12), and "Le Tableau" (4.17) complete the series. The mathematical regularity by which this theme recurs is doubled by allusions within the prologues to the other tales in this series. In "Le Psautier," the second in the series, the author announces that this will be the last tale about nuns. In "Les Lunettes," he recalls his previous promise, but allows himself one more, swearing that this will be the last. Of course, it is not; "Le Tableau" is. The ordering of independent tales in the anthology mimes the passage of time within a regularly recurring and, therefore, seemingly predictable mathematical pattern, while the authorial prologues allude to previous tales in the series, but pretend not to know what tales will follow.

As Jean-Pierre Collinet has shown in his study of the *Contes*, the authorial prologues take several forms, the most interesting of which "double the principal *récit* with a first tale" ("La Matière et l'art du prologue" 234; my translation). If this tendency were pushed a bit further, "the accessory would become the principal, would suffice to itself and make the rest from then on superfluous" (235). "Le Tableau" is in some respects the illustration of the limits of this tendency. While there is no included tale that displaces the "main" tale, the prologue itself takes on certain distinguishing features of the tale genre, displacing and deferring the main tale in such a way that the relation between what readers take for accessory and principal is inverted.[8] The first sign of this inversion is the enigmatic title of the tale, which, the reader learns, has nothing at all to do with the nuns' story (presumably the main tale), but refers to the object of imitation. As such, the title names the authorial prologue rather than the main tale as in all the rest of La Fontaine's tales. The tale to be told will be the reading of a painting. In fact, "prologue" in the case of "Le Tableau" is a misnomer. It is rather a parasitic, secondary discourse that forces itself on its readers by hypocritically suppressing for reasons of decorum exactly what they want to see. The "prologue" thus mimes the functioning of the tale itself and in so doing deflects the reader's attention from the "primary," the nuns' story, to the ancillary, the tale of the telling of a tale. This deflection is, however, essential, since, as we will see, without a certain self-censorship (suppressions and attenuations operated through authorial intervention), the tale could not be told in the "first" place.

"Le Tableau" opens by presenting itself as the author's response to a wager, or the inauguration of a contract between author-narrator and a certain implied readership:

On m'engage à conter d'une manière honnête
Le sujet d'un de ces tableaux
Sur lesquels on met des rideaux.
Il me faut tirer de ma tête
Nombre de traits nouveaux, piquants et délicats,
Qui disent et ne disent pas,
Et qui soient entendus sans notes
Des Agnès même les plus sottes:
Ce n'est pas coucher gros, ces extrêmes Agnès
Sont oiseaux qu'on ne vit jamais.

    The narrator cites his source for this particular tale by gesturing to a painting that must be covered by curtains. Of course, the French indefinite pronoun *on* seems to point to and conceal a human referent in a way the English passive voice cannot do. The referential gesture to a particular painting presumed to be "real" and even to a class of paintings hidden by curtains from the eyes of the uninitiated is unmistakable. From the beginning, "Le Tableau" stages three representational levels. It purports to be the verbal representation of a pictorial representation, itself the pictorial moment of an "original" narrative.

    There is clearly no stable reference outside of this mimetic play. This double distancing of the central tale from "reality" contrasts neatly with the framing "prologue," whose deictics gesture to an extratextual reality, a real painting, "un de ces tableaux / Sur lesquels on met des rideaux." The text invests heavily in creating the illusion of realism in the prologue to the point that it is altogether surprising that three centuries of careful researchers have not proposed pictorial sources for this tale.[9] The decision to represent this tale as the imitation of a painting has the effect of stabilizing the mimesis through reference to a material object. Read on the most naively referential level, the prologue presupposes a doubly inaccessible world where curtained paintings are displayed and the curtains opened only for a certain elite. This peculiar naturalizing fiction, however, mirrors that of the novella (*nouvelle*), which purported to tell the true, that is, secret story behind the official histories and aristocratic façades of Louis XIV's reign. As Erica Harth has shown (129), the subversion of the *ut pictura poesis* system is closely linked to the distinction made at this time between histories and stories (both *histoires* in French), novels (*romans*) and novellas (*nouvelles*). The *vraisemblance* of the framing device parallels that of the novella, which told the secrets of groups ultimately unknowable to seventeenth-century readers and, especially, to the well-bred ladies to whom the tale is explicitly addressed.

"Le Tableau" is thus first of all a two-part narrative that tells the story of the transmission and reception of a forbidden object of pleasure (the content of the painting) and in the telling of this story, in fulfilling the conditions of the initial contract, will reveal what is ordinarily hidden. It is significant that the "prologue" is itself cast in the mold of the tale. There is a plot, a narrative program to be carried out: Will the author-subject succeed in revealing this pornographic painting to the implied readers ("belles")? There are allies (the Muses and Apollo) and opponents (Censors). Indeed, this prologue meets the conditions for what Marc Eli Blanchard has called a "paranarrative" because it foregrounds elements that contribute to the impression that what is being read is already the reading of a reading (129). However, this paranarrative functions negatively by asserting figures of suppression, thereby betraying its own action and setting itself up for eventual failure.

The painting as painting is not directly receivable by La Fontaine's implied reader, since the conditions imposed by the literary contract specify "d'une manière honnête."[10] *Bienséances*, the bugbear of classical literary theory, imposes itself. As has been often pointed out, classical Horatian *decorum* is not at all the same thing as French seventeenth-century *bienséances*. *Decorum*, which meant, for Horace, appropriateness or specific conformity in the representation of character, physique, gesture, and so on (Lee, *Ut Pictura Poesis* 35), has come to mean by the late seventeenth century acceptability to the standards of taste and morality of the dominant culture (Harth 29; 96). This shift in the evaluation of mimesis implies no less than a reorientation of the artistic enterprise. Values of "pure" imitation must be tempered by specific conditions of reception. *Bienséances* in this sense is *decorum* from the point of view of the reader and entails a theory of reading of which "Le Tableau" might be seen as the allegory.

This shift in emphasis in the evaluation of mimesis from the appropriateness of words to things to the appropriateness to a cultural code situated outside of the literary experience is mirrored in the structure of seventeenth-century criticism. As Hugh M. Davidson (142) has observed, when the great dramatic authors of the period wrote prefaces to the printed versions of works that had already been performed and commented on, their intent was less to expose a theory than to react to their audience's reaction. Hence the duplicitous nature of critical *pro*-logues and *pre*-faces, whose prefixes imply priority but which are in fact tertiary discourses, commentaries on absent commentaries, that nevertheless proclaim their temporal and logical priority in the production of the work. In the prologues to La Fontaine's tales, this critical distance is lacking, but its structure is imposed on a literary form that has not in fact been tried, so to speak, on the arbiters of *bienséances*. The temporal structure of the practice of literary criticism is mimed through the fiction of the painting. In the case of "Le Tableau," the guarantee of the author's efficacy in predicting and encoding his audience's reaction and in thematizing it in a secondary narrative that is itself a kind of tale is the fact of the prior censorship of his object of imitation; this painting is covered by curtains.[11]

In purporting to be the literary description of a painting, "Le Tableau," like Cupid's tapestry studied in the previous chapter, exhibits certain characteristics of an *ekphrasis*, the reading in a literary text of a visual work of art accorded prior existence as object and presumed to have a meaning that the literary text will make explicit.[12] This is the etymological meaning of the word, from the Greek "to speak out," "to tell in full." This technique is as old as literature itself, since its most prestigious example is Homer's description of Achilles's shield in Book 18 of the *Iliad*, to which La Fontaine will allude near the end of "Le Tableau." As a secondary reading and the representation of a representation, an *ekphrasis* necessarily thematizes a certain displacement from the "original" conditions of creation and reception of the visual artwork. This displacement leaves its trace in the text in the form of a parallel discourse of artifice and technique on one hand, and reading and interpretation on the other. In an *ekphrasis* the visual and linguistic sign systems are related to each other, suprisingly perhaps, in ways that point out differences in the two sign systems. Giving voice to a mute painting does not, within the *ut pictura poesis* system, render mimesis itself problematic but serves to demonstrate that any represented ultimately refers to a pre-representational signified, that is, truth or nature. However, as a representation of a representation, *ekphrasis* does assume an additional burden of *vraisemblance* with respect to the integrity of the imitated object as object.[13]

The example that follows the initial exposition of the literary problem posed by the curtained painting attempts to reduce to hypocrisy on the part of the viewer or reader any difference in what is acceptable to the eye or the ear, and thereby emphasizes the ludic nature of the literary contract. The decorously told description of a pornographic painting is a literary *tour de force* and only that, since in a world without hypocrisy the painting could be displayed and viewed. The narrator makes this point by citing "Catullus," a classical, and therefore, in the game the text is playing, an irreprochable, authority. The particular example chosen, however, is the most audacious possible.

> Toute matrone sage, à ce que dit Catulle,
> Regarde volontiers le gigantesque don
> Fait au fruit de Vénus par la main de Junon:
> A ce plaisant objet si quelqu'une recule,
> > Cette quelqu'une dissimule.
> Ce principe posé, pourquoi plus de scrupule,
> Pourquoi moins de licence aux oreilles qu'aux yeux?
> Puisqu'on le veut ainsi, je ferai de mon mieux.

The allusion to "Catullus" has a double function in the reader's decoding of the narrator's example.[14] "Catullus" is, of course, an authority in the classical sense. "Catullus" lends prestige to author and argument. On the other hand, for the seventeenth-century reader the allusion to Roman poetry connotes licentiousness in speech, whether or not the reader has any practical familiarity with the particular text to which the narrator alludes. Boileau (167) gives this cliché its most perfect literary expression and at the same time suggests the most common understanding of French classicism as attenuation:

> Le Latin dans les mots brave l'honnesteté
> Mais le lecteur françois veut être respecté.
> Du moindre sens impur la liberté l'outrage
> Si la pudeur des mots n'en adoucit l'image.

Readers might thus infer that a faithful citation of "Catullus" would include proper terms not allowed by contemporary standards of decorum. In failing to deal with this connotation, the narrator devalues Catullus as proper authority for his argument. Licentiousness in speech is simultaneously connoted and negated in the periphrasis that follows as the rewriting of an unmentionable term. The text seeks to have it both ways by asserting its right on the authority of Catullus to represent the unmentionable and by veiling through periphrasis and allusion the represented object in such a way that it is impossible to decide exactly what is represented in this tale, a god, a god's statue, or a mortal male. The representation of the unmentionable here works like an *ekphrasis* by activating the *topos* of artifice and technique at its most primary level, the *deus*, or in this case *dea, artifex* theme (Curtius 544-46).

According to tradition, Priapus, Venus's son, owed his deformity to Juno's jealousy (ed. Régnier 5: 580n). In La Fontaine's tale, "punishment" becomes a "gift," but the essential is that the emblem of masculinity is represented as an object of exchange between women. The implication is that women need never fear seeing their own handiwork. The Roman matron, of course, never gazed on the god Priapus but on statues, or *priapi*, that graced every Roman garden. The religious or even archaeological sense of the myth will most likely be entirely lost on the seventeenth-century or contemporary reader whose imagination supposedly naturalizes the mimesis through reference to the real world. This example restages the representational levels on which "Le Tableau" as a whole is built. Rather than name the "pleasing object," the text conflates the myth of the god Priapus's origins with visual representations of the god and leaves the reader open to a very improper "referential" naturalization.

The narrator of the prologue has just hypocritically asserted the theoretical equality of ear and eye by condemning as hypocrisy any difference between visual and verbal representations. He is left with unimpressive reasons for pursuing his literary project: "Puisqu'on le veut ainsi." At the point where critical justification is at its weakest, the narrator mobilizes his most powerful image, that of the veil.[15] He proposes to veil his tale in gauze, thereby creating a third term in his representational scheme and, I think, proposing a serious alternative to one accepted view of French classicism as mere attenuation.

>Nuls traits à découvert n'auront ici de place;
>Tout y sera voilé, mais de gaze, et si bien
>Que je crois qu'on n'en perdra rien.

The gauze veil is from the outset a highly ambiguous figure whose ambiguity cannot be reduced either to suppression or to revelation. As a variant of the curtains that prevent access to the pornographic painting, the veil does indeed figure suppression, censorship, and hypocrisy. It stands between viewer (the double of the implied reader) and painting, thereby inhibiting unmediated perception of a presumed underlying content. And yet this veil hides nothing. If anything, it points to where the reader should look. As a surface protection of latent meaning, the veil is deliberately revealing, and as a textual metaphor, the veil constitutes before our eyes the very thing it both reveals and conceals. Indeed, this veil is beginning to resemble what Derrida after Mallarmé has taught us to call a *hymen*, a space between, text and textile, a figure of innocence and violation.[16] The veil figures mutually incompatible, even paradoxical, meanings, both suppression and revelation, each of which needs to be activated at different levels in the text, usually by negation of its opposite.

It seems that through its structure of interposition and (partial) transparency, the figure of the veil also curiously resembles one of the founding images of classical discourse, namely Galileo's telescope, which Timothy Reiss has considered the image of the classical reorientation of the sign: "The telescope may therefore be taken as a fair representation of what happened to the linguistic sign itself, increasingly defined as an arbitrarily selected transparent instrument placed between concept and object" (26).[17] This is also a fair description of the veil, the difference residing in the degree of transparency. Reiss finds it symptomatic of what has happened in and to discourse that this image could be safely reversed in *Il Cannochiale aristotelico* (1654), the title of Emanuele Tesauro's treatise on rhetoric and poetics, in which metaphor is itself a telescope. La Fontaine's readers are already familiar with at least one literary avatar of the telescope through the fable of the animal on the moon ("Un Animal dans la lune," *Fables* 7.17), which takes as its point of departure a general reflection on the truth and falsity of what vision can tell us in order to tell the anecdote of a mouse caught between the lenses of a telescope aimed at the moon. This anecdote is itself the pretext for an even more general reflection that involves no less than all scientific knowledge, philosophy, the fine arts, and the social order as guaranteed by the monarchy. For Pierre Zoberman, who justly cites this fable in his study on the relation between seeing, knowing, and speaking in the classical episteme, this fable is symptomatic of the privilege, and also the discredit, accorded the eye in seventeenth-century rhetoric, whose "ambition, or justification, is to render the matter of discourse directly visible" (Zoberman 410; my translation).

Within the discursive system in elaboration, any metalinguistic discourse seems inevitably to fall back on pictorial metaphors (Bennington, "Réappropriations" 505). For the classical rhetoricians, the role of speech is to copy the mental painting one carries in one's head. This model was, of course, not universally accepted. Pascal and the theorists of Port Royal explictly contested it (Lyons, "Speaking" 168-69). The first chapter of the *Logic of Port Royal* denounces this dangerous metaphor with an insistence that seems almost obsessive, to the point that in denouncing it, the metaphor is asserted by the discourse that attempts to refute it. What is taking place in the metalinguistic discourse of the classical rhetoricians is the invasion of all metaphors by hypotyposis, a particular sort of metaphor that Du Marsais defines in the following way:

> L'Hypotypose est un mot grec qui signifie *image, tableau*. C'est lorsque, dans les descriptions, on peint les faits dont on parle comme si ce qu'on

dit était actuellement devant les yeux; on montre, pour ainsi dire, ce qu'on ne fait que raconter; on donne en quelque sorte l'original pour la copie, les objets pour les tableaux. (Du Marsais 110)

As Du Marsais's definition shows, the larger problem of figuration is already implicit in the metalinguistic discourse of the classical period. Only a trope can restore the "original" in place of the "copy," thereby creating the illusion of presence of the referent while occluding its own materiality.

The figure of the veil, however much it owes to figures of vision as model of all modes of perception, resists recuperation and naturalization as merely or even primarily visual by insisting on the partialness, the fragmentary nature of what is perceived across the veil. In much the same way as in Baudelaire's "Correspondances," the problematics of the poetic enterprise articulating poetry and poetics is revealed in its temporal indeterminacy ("[...] Laissent *parfois* sortir de confuses paroles"), the veil is indeterminately transparent, or indeterminately opaque. There always remains a textual residue, a play of signifiers that inhibit complete recuperation of the linguistic and specifically the textual by the visual. Thus the veil begun as a visual metaphor becomes the figure of the text.

Readers of "Le Tableau" may begin to perceive what is happening thanks to a play on words authorized by the playful nature of the genre. The figure of the veil gains in complexity and interest in this tale about nuns, since the veil is their distinguishing article of dress and the sign par excellence of their difference. The text thus plays on the meanings *veil* may have, as nun's veil or as curtains covering a painting, both on their way to becoming a powerful textual metaphor. In "Le Tableau" the nun's veil interposes itself between body and eye, "l'œil du jour" or some lover's eye, in much the same way the curtains hid the painting:

> En mille endroits nichait l'Amour,
> Sous une guimpe, un voile, et sous un scapulaire,
> Sous ceci, sous cela, que voit peu l'œil du jour
> Si celui du galant ne l'appelle au mystère.

The text evokes the bodily presence of the two nuns as they await their lover by displaying the veil and its vestimentary variants within a spatial relationship ("underneath") whose importance is signaled by the repetition of "*sous*." Here again we see the veil read in two mutually incompatible ways as a sign of separation from the world and a surface to be penetrated. This peculiarly revealing concealment or concealed revelation, while originating in visual metaphor, cannot lend itself to visualization as a picture.

Insofar as it is the description of a veiled painting, "Le Tableau" claims to be a kind of *ekphrasis*, but one that allows suppression of those elements in the text that could be naturalized by pictorialization. In fact, Hagstrum's criteria for evaluating the pictorial in literature (Hagstrum xxii) provide a checklist for what "Le Tableau" does not do. (1) It is not translatable into a painting. (2) Its details are not ordered in a picturable way. (3) There is no reduction of motion to stasis, and (4) meaning does not seem to arise exclusively or even primarily from picturable detail. In "Le Tableau," references to the materiality of the painting as artifact, including those that relate to the spatial disposition of figures within the picture, are for the most part suppressed. Where texts written within the ekphrastic tradition (Cupid's tapestry in *Psyché* for example) generate paranarratives of production, technique, or spatial display (Blanchard), "Le Tableau" substitutes a parallel discourse of concealment with respect to space, and temporization with respect to time. In fact, everything seems to be happening in this tale as if, because the figure of the veil necessarily connotes suppression and given the nature of the literary contract between author and reader, the painting's meaning cannot be entirely suppressed, and something must be. That something turns out to be "picturability," a kind of virtual hypotyposis, the very figure that makes the veil itself intelligible in the first place.

The tale now proceeds by a series of detours, substitutions, and temporizations that distance the reader from the "painting" from which the tale is presumably derived by emphasizing specifically nonpicturable detail. A single explicit gesture to figures within the painting paradoxically points out the eventual failure of this tale to be reconstructed visually as a picture. Near the end of the authorial prologue, the narrator restates the theoretical equality of ear and eye and the hypocrisy of having to veil for the ear what the eye willingly seeks. He then proleptically evokes the "picture" in a single verse:

> Je veux, quoi qu'il en soit, expliquer à des belles
> Cette chaise rompue, et ce rustre tombé.

These deictics ("*cette* chaise"; "*ce* rustre") are signs to the reader of the presumed presence of the author-viewer before the painting. A visual moment that authorizes the mention of the broken chair before the chair has been broken in the literary retelling of the tale is thus assumed from the very beginning.

The author then appeals to the Muses, but, as they are virgins, he rejects them as inappropriate adjuvants in his narrative program and settles on Apollo as his helper.[18] The paranarrative, now possessing a more or less complete actantial cast, closes by referring once again to the object to be communicated to the "belles": "C'est assez raisonner; venons à la peinture."

The word *peinture* is so heavily involved in the figural interplay assumed by the *ut pictura poesis* system that confining its range of meanings exclusively to "painting" would be anachronistic. Its range of meanings includes the act of painting or of describing, as well as the object, visual or verbal, that is the result of that activity (Furetière, *peinture*). Of course, prior reference to a "real" painting orients the reader's interpretation toward the object hidden behind the curtains. However, the narrator does not in fact get to the painting. The moment when the painting will have to be revealed is deferred in a rather long digression (103 verses, or 17 verses short of half the tale) that involves such unpicturable detail as the substitution of the awaited lover by the "mazet," an avatar of Masetto da Lamporecchio, who was himself on his way to another lover. The tale spins on waiting for the bachelor, who, like Godot, never arrives, and therefore could never be represented figurally in a painting. The awaited bachelor thus represents an essentially unpicturable structural absence, the object of the nuns' desire, who, by not arriving at the prepared feast, will be replaced by the first comer. As we have seen, this substitution in the plot level of the tale curiously figures the intertextual displacement implied by the double source, first in Aretino and then in Boccaccio. The text thus establishes a fundamental parallelism between the reading and writing of the tale on one level and the movement, presence, and absence of characters on another.

The detour that brings the "mazet" to the nuns in place of the awaited lover thus brings the reader, some hundred verses later, back to the painting: "Ici la peinture commence." Of course, the painting or its description does not in any sense "begin" here; it is not conceived as a *punctum temporis*, which the preceding digression served only to circumstance, nor are there gestures to the spatial disposition of figures within the painting. In fact, the "beginning" of the painting "here" marks the end of the tale in the neutral narratorial voice and a return to the paranarrative. What is behind the veil is evoked in a conversation between author and Apollo on how best to explain what cannot be plainly told.

This segment of the paranarrative in which the author seeks help in accomplishing his task by requesting the intervention of Apollo provides a route back into the tale proper by making the conventional personification of Love do double service in both narrative and paranarrative:

> J'ai tort d'ériger un fripon
> En maître des cérémonies.
> Dès qu'il entre en une maison,
> Règles et lois en sont bannies:
> Sa fantaisie est sa raison.
> Le voilà qui rompt tout [. . .].

These verses serve equally well on two levels, either as a more or less conventional allegory of the effects of love on characters in the tale or as an allegory of the representation of love, the same game we observed in Cupid's tapestry. The place of these verses in the commentary of author and Apollo and the metalinguistic connotations of "règles et lois," so important for classical literary theory, suggest that these verses contain an explicit poetics of the inexplicit tale. The concomitant desire to represent physical love decorously within the "rules" and the impossibility of so doing necessitates a ruptured narrative and engenders the paranarrative. The transition between the dialogue with Apollo in the paranarrative and the tale proper turns precisely on the word *rompre*: "Le voilà qui rompt tout [. . .]." The past participle of *rompre*, we have seen, has already been used to evoke proleptically the broken chair in the picture. Breaking the rules of *bienséances* and breaking the chair are represented as the results of more or less the same agency.

The penultimate movement in "Le Tableau" involves an extraordinary extended parallel with the Trojan War, evokes Achilles's armor as described in Book 18 of the *Iliad*, and ends with the famous verses that, contrary to the thesis on which the tale has been built, disclaim the virtual identity of the verbal and the visual in the production and reception of a represented object. The Trojan War theme enters the tale as a burlesque in which the two nuns fight over which will have the peasant. The sexual inversion of the situation is explicitly cited ("Un pitaud [. . .] tint ici lieu d'Hélène"), and, once again, production of the tale as text is seen as a recasting of roles, a substitution operated between texts. The war theme is then used to evoke the nuns' nudity by negating "armor," a metonym of the war theme. Another authorial aside to his female readers serves as a sign that the veil has been once again imposed, that there is something "there" to be understood that the reader must decode: "Belles, vous m'entendez; je ne dirai pas plus."

As if further demonstration were needed, this passage illustrates the subtlety of what Leo Spitzer has called La Fontaine's art of transition:

> L'habit de guerre de Vénus
> Est plein de choses admirables!
> Les cyclopes aux membres nus
> Forgent peu de harnois qui lui soient comparables:
> Celui du preux Achille aurait été plus beau,
> Si Vulcan eût dessus gravé notre tableau.

In keeping with the vestimentary code I have already examined, the nuns' nudity is called the battle dress of Venus. The term is another literary veil protecting and displaying the nuns' nudity while protecting and displaying the act of representing an improper subject. As in the initial example of Priapus, the literary representation of an object of visual art, even in an extended and unpicturable metaphor, seems inevitably to activate the *topos* of *deus artifex*. The divine armorers made armor that cannot be compared to that of Venus. This is, of course, literally true, since only in this extraordinary conceit can nudity, lack of dress, be compared to battle garb. Figuratively, this is high praise for the beauty of Venus and of the similarly clothed nuns. In passing, I should note the burlesque "Homeric" epithet "cyclopes aux membres nus" in which the veiled seme "nudity" is applied to the Cyclopes rather than to Venus or the two nuns. Again, the essential but unmentionable signified is deflected from its "proper" place to a point where it can be simultaneously absent from the description and still present in the text. Once the artisan Cyclopes have been mentioned, it seems almost natural to evoke their most famous artistic production, the paragon of fine workmanship, Achilles's armor, whose description in *Iliad* 18 is also the paragon of all *ekphraseis*. In a remarkable construction *en abyme*, the narrator declares that even Achilles's shield would have been more beautiful had Vulcan engraved "our painting" on it. This impertinent, playful comparison with the most prestigious of classic texts is so violently at odds with readers' expectations of order and propriety in the literary world that one might very likely suspect parody.[19] This comparison should perhaps not be seen only as an ironic aside meant merely to plumb the profound distance between the Homeric epic at one end of the classical hierarchy and the verse tale at the other. Suggesting the possibility of reopening the Homeric text and the divinely wrought armor to retrospective change of any kind, burlesque or serious, is in itself theoretically interesting. This possibility defines the space in which all arts of imitation may be inscribed.

La Fontaine's retrospective desire to improve Achilles's shield can also be examined with respect to the way this particular text was read in the classical period. We find it exactly in the center of a three-century-long controversy on the relation of the literary to the visual. The point of contention on which Scaliger the Elder, Perrault, and later Lessing entered the fray was precisely to what extent Homer had described in the Book 18 *ekphrasis* more than could be engraved on a real shield; that is, whether the *ekphrasis* was in excess of the limitations of the material support (Lessing 98). Despite modern critical prejudice against counterfactual statements in general (Hirsch), the counterfactual correction or improvement of the Homeric *ekphrasis* in "Le Tableau" can be understood in several ways. It might represent a degree of authorial wishful thinking. "Our painting" in Homer would have authorized for all time just the sort of poem "Le Tableau" might have been, had it not been necessary to veil it. On another level, the distinction between visual object and its verbal representation is further eroded. To what does "our painting" refer? To the painting behind the curtains or to the tale entitled "Le Tableau"? Finally, the Homeric *ekphrasis*, commonly considered a totalizing metaphor for all human experience ("la grandiose allégorie de la création" [Buffière 157]), is incomplete, therefore less beautiful, for lack of a representation of sexuality. Even a burlesque episode like the nuns' story might have sufficed.

These rather odd considerations preface the verses on which the reputation of "Le Tableau" as *ars poetica* is built:

> Or ai-je des nonnains mis en vers l'aventure,
> Mais non avec des traits dignes de l'action;
> Et comme celle-ci déchet dans la peinture,
> La peinture déchet dans ma description:
> Les mots et les couleurs ne sont choses pareilles;
> Ni les yeux ne sont les oreilles.

There are no surprises here for modern readers, accustomed as they are to the most durable of critical oppositions, that of narration and description.[20] But as we have seen, this opposition, in the late seventeenth century or for that matter in the centuries that preceded it, was by no means self-evident. In "Le Tableau" the distinction emerges as the result of the failure of the attempt to reveal in language what could also have been revealed in a painting. One kind of failure engenders another kind of success. The success of the paranarrative in telling the tale of the veiling of the painting depends precisely on the failure of the narrative proper to appropriate fully the content of the painting. The veil, at once emblem and technique of the practice by which the two narratives are articulated, thus becomes a wedge in the structure of representation itself, indistinctly and indeterminately partitioning off what had been complementary practices.

On one level, of course, La Fontaine's discovery that the eyes are not the ears is no discovery at all, but a succinct restatement and demonstration of the already well-known distinction between the arts of time and the arts of space. What is interesting in "Le Tableau" is less what it says about seventeenth-century theory as a set of discursive statements than what it does in and to the *ut pictura poesis* representational system. It effectively allegorizes the act of reading a (fictive) painting and encodes that reading in a paranarrative. In so doing, the limits and contradictions of the *ut pictura poesis* system are figured in the veil, which becomes in the text an unvisualizable figure of the text itself. In adapting the strategy of the veil, "Le Tableau" inverts the central problem of representation inherent in the *ut pictura poesis* system. As the correspondence between words and the hidden image is essentially unknowable to the reader, the question is no longer how the verbal effaces itself in deference to what is outside itself but how the visual (in this case the "painting") is effaced in its purported representation in language. The veil is the trace of that effacement. But the veil as authorial strategy for revelation is meaningless without a motivation for the repression the veil also implies. As Michel Foucault has clearly seen, what has consistently been taken for the repression of sexuality in Western bourgeois culture since the seventeenth century is doubled by a parallel movement, the task of putting sexuality into discourse. The veil figures the double movement of repression and revelation of sexuality, which can now be understood as complementary projects. By finding the language to reveal what must be hidden and by figuring this process in a visual metaphor that soon loses its grounding in vision, "Le Tableau" displays and, in a sense, puts into question this task at a moment very near the historical inception of modern discourse.

Conclusion

In this excursion through a handful of works by La Fontaine, I set out to demonstrate the importance and interest of reading and writing in La Fontaine. In reflecting on the text, I wanted to consider the role of the implied reader and, also, the role of the history of readings that have shaped our modern sense of "La Fontaine." I proceeded under the assumption of a general intertextuality, namely that the "text" includes its gloss as inscribed by generations of readers, commentators, and critics and that La Fontaine, as reader and writer himself, was working under much the same conditions with his inherited sources and influences. I have thus pointed to La Fontaine's novel, *Psyché*, and to a certain number of fables and tales that explicitly reflect on reading and writing through the *mise en scène* of acts of reading and writing and through very special moments when the logic of the text finds its figure in a body, a brain, a hieroglyphic, a veil, a labyrinth, a name, a painting. This essay might thus have gone on happily reading La Fontaine, uncovering other textual figures.

In retrospect, a number of fables and tales I have not discussed offer possibilities for exploring seventeenth-century textuality with La Fontaine. I might have wished to include a reading of "La Vie d'Esope le phrygien," La Fontaine's prose introduction to the first collection of the *Fables*. I could not, however, add a word to Louis Marin's reading ("Le Récit originaire"), nor for that matter to his brilliant study of "Le Pouvoir des Fables" (*Fables* 8.4), an essential fable in the canon of fables of the text. The *Nouveaux contes*, which close with "Le Tableau," are particularly rich in textual figures. "Le Cas de conscience" (*Contes* 4.4) merits particular attention as a text that displays the process of putting sexuality into discourse.[1] "Le Psautier" (*Contes* 4.7) means a sacred book before it became in La Fontaine's tale by this name another textile, a variant of the veil, and finally the sign of a sexual escapade. Fables that explicitly treat problems of interpretation, such as "Testament expliqué par Esope" (*Fables* 2.20), the closing fable of Book 2, might have been profitably explored. More attention might be focused on inscription fables such as the curious double fable "Le Loup, la Chèvre et le Chevreau" and "Le Loup, la Mère et l'Enfant" (*Fables* 4.15-16), which I treated briefly in Chapter 5, or "Le Vieillard et les Trois Jeunes Hommes" (*Fables* 11.8), in which the fable and its inscription become one.

Even within my narrower area of concern, I do not pretend to have treated, or even discovered, all of La Fontaine's figures of the text. Other figures might motivate a look at other works by La Fontaine. As Bernard Beugnot has shown ("Spécularités"), La Fontaine fully exploits the figure of the mirror in *Psyché* and also in "L'Homme et son image" (*Fables* 1.11), a fable dedicated to La Rochefoucauld. Pierre Malandain makes much of the wind as intertextual operator in the *Fables*. A more detailed look at wind fables might dispel our contemporary prejudice for static models of the text and against fluid metaphors (Malandain 71-80). I hope my reading of the windy soul in "La Laitière et le Pot au lait" (Chapter 3) is a step in that direction. As Zobeidah Youssef has shown, water images abound in La Fontaine. They might offer a particular interest for a playful poet named "la fontaine." Does the poet by this name sign his texts in water?

All branches of poetics could no doubt be enriched through their contact with La Fontaine. Proper names, as I hope to have shown here and elsewhere, are for moderns, as they were in a very different way for Champollion, the royal road to understanding textuality ("Naming Names"; "Naming the Cid"). La Fontaine might be an excellent point of departure for a general study of the poetics of the name in the seventeenth century.[2] Thanks to the scholarship of La Fontaine's editors and commentators from Régnier to Fumaroli, we are very well informed on La Fontaine's textual sources. However, more work on intertextuality, on the reader's necessary perception that the text is doing something in and to another text, is called for. The particular problem in the seventeenth century of citation, the embedding of one text in another, has recently received attention in Nicholas Cronk's "The Singular Voice: Monologism and French Classical Discourse." One might usefully apply to La Fontaine his contention that the "classical author is a *dialogiste malgré lui*, condemned to having to write dialogically while pretending not to" (194).

Finally, for serious students of La Fontaine, the program of inquiry proposed by Richard Danner in his *Patterns of Irony* remains. Danner insightfully and methodically demonstrated the overwhelming importance of irony in La

Conclusion 111

Fontaine with respect to three critical articulations, namely texture, closure, and architecture. Other considerations of La Fontaine of whatever theoretical inclination must take account of Danner's agenda. As far as this study is concerned, I need not here reconsider the first of these, since texture and all that is implied in the term has been my major focus. However, in a study interested in textuality as such, the question of the arrangement of fragments, of individual fables, into wholes, the question of the architecture, or "architexture," of the *Fables* and *Contes*, ought to be asked, since the most immediate sign of their textuality is their disposition in books. It is curious that in the history of the reading of La Fontaine there is a certain lack of interest in this question until fairly recently, until, perhaps, (post-)modern reflections on textuality have questioned the status of the book itself (Derrida, "La Fin du livre et le commencement de l'écriture," *De la grammatologie* 15-41). In his review of Danner's *Patterns*, Henri Peyre, for example, called Danner's interest in the order of the fables in each book "a pseudo-problem" (119-20). I would maintain that it is not now a "pseudo-problem," although at one time it might have been.

Since Georges Couton suggested in "Le Livre épicurien" (290) that the best way to read the fables is book by book, the book as organizing principle of the fables has become a major focus of critical attention.[3] Despite any number of arguments advanced in favor of the coherence of La Fontaine's books of fables, one is left with the suspicion that what is really at issue is the nature of the book itself. A book, even a book of fables (so the common thread of the argument goes) ought to embody an idea, a theme, a subject that the critic can discover and describe. We know, more or less, how to read individual fables and tales; how to read books of fables is another matter entirely. Indeed, La Fontaine's collections of fables and tales betray two simultaneous and contradictory movements: the book as sign of their continuity, order, coherence and the individually numbered fables and tales that remain discrete, discontinuous, self-sustaining.[4] Perhaps the time has come to ask ingeniously why the fables and tales are in books in the first place, in the same way that Jean Mesnard asked why Pascal's *Pensées* are in fragments ("Pourquoi les *Pensées* de Pascal se présentent-elles sous forme de fragments?"). We should not be satisfied with the obvious answer (because Phaedrus collected his fables into books) any more than Mesnard was satisfied with the obvious answer for Pascal.

Even provisional responses to questions on the internal architecture of the *Fables* and *Contes*, like the one I proposed for the *Nouveaux contes* in

Chapter 7, inevitably evoke the problem of closure, which Barbara Herrnstein Smith neatly defines in this way:

> Closure occurs when the concluding portion of a poem creates in the reader a sense of appropriate cessation. It announces and justifies the absence of further development; it reinforces the feeling of finality, completion, and composure which we value in works of art; and it gives ultimate unity and coherence to the reader's experience of the poem by providing a point from which all the preceding elements may be viewed comprehensively and their relations grasped as part of a significant design. (36)

La Fontaine's magnificent enterprise, the twelve books of fables, seems to end well with "Le Juge Arbitre, l'Hospitalier et le Solitaire" (*Fables* 12.29):

> Cette leçon sera la fin de ces Ouvrages:
> Puisse-t-elle être utile aux siècles à venir!
> Je la présente aux Rois, je la propose aux Sages:
>   Par où saurais-je mieux finir?

Bernard Beugnot is not so certain: "Le recueil des *Fables* ne se clôt pas sur une élévation, mais si replie sur le secret et l'intimité d'une conscience poétique qui découpe, dans un univers sans Dieu, l'espace étroit de son rêve" ("Autour d'un texte" 301). La Fontaine, it seems, makes trouble with endings. As Danner has well demonstrated, closural effects within individual fables are susceptible to ironic deformation. I have discussed other closural difficulties, for example the unending embedded stories in *Psyché* that strangely mirror intertextual displacements, or the rhetorical (?) question that closes "Démocrite et les Abdéritains." I would suggest at this point that closural effects seem particularly troubled at strategic points within books of fables and tales. What, for example, are we to make of "Les Animaux malades de la peste" (*Fables* 7.1), the first fable in the second collection? A universally admired masterpiece, this fable nonetheless lacks closure as described by Smith. The fable opens with a powerful poetic evocation of the plague, heavy with overtones of Sophocles and Lucretius. It ends with the cynical sacrifice of an (almost) innocent victim. Although the New Criticism has trained us not to ask unanswerable questions, what reader does not want to know the unwritten ending? Will the plague lift? The moral, even theological, weight of the fable is left

Conclusion

hanging on this inconclusive ending. We are left to wonder at the meaning of an opening fable that does not quite conclude.

In this study, I have tried to show to what extent La Fontaine continues to offer a wealth of evidence for the study of poetics, the theory of reading and of textuality. At the beginning of this project I asked rhetorically what remained to be said about La Fontaine. I will count this work a success if, because of the nature of the questions I have put to La Fontaine's work, more now remains to be said than when I began.

Notes

INTRODUCTION

[1] This approach to literature, although not my own, has certainly produced some interesting results within La Fontaine studies. Jane Merino-Morais's *Différence et répétition dans les "Contes" de La Fontaine*, for example, is a convincing application of A. J. Greimas's narrative grammar to La Fontaine's verse tales.

[2] This too brief survey is not meant to pass over the work of Leo Spitzer, Odette de Mourgues, Margaret Guitton, Nathan Gross, Philip Wadsworth, John Lapp, Georges Couton, Marcel Gutwirth, and many others who have written illuminatingly on La Fontaine, especially Jean-Pierre Collinet, the dean of La Fontaine scholars, whose recent collection of essays *La Fontaine en amont et en aval* (1988) supplements his masterly *Le Monde littéraire*.

For a more complete *état présent* of critical readings of La Fontaine, see Marie-Odile Sweetser's recent *La Fontaine*. Her own penetrating analyses of La Fontaine's works, along with her sympathetic reading of other, primarily American, students of La Fontaine, provide an indispensable introduction to La Fontaine's work for scholar and student alike.

[3] See, for example, my "Transtextual Traps," an attempt to apply Marin's trap model to "Le Rat et l'Huître" (*Fables* 8.9).

[4] The quotation and the notion of a few handfuls of absolutely essential terms is from Emile Benveniste's *Problèmes de linguistique générale* (336).

[5] Among recent studies on the nature of the text in the classical period, I would like to acknowledge the recent work of Francis Barker, Jonathan Goldberg, and especially Geoffrey Bennington. Barker's views on textuality and corporeality will be discussed at some length in Chapter 2.

[6] This is precisely the critical countermove from which Richard Danner (*Patterns of Irony* 31) had to insulate himself in dealing with irony in La Fontaine.

He relies on textual analysis as a means of avoiding the accusation of having created a "self-confirming hypothesis."

[7] For a powerful critique of Barthes's treatment of the dissolution of the subject, implicit in this definition of the text, see Nancy K. Miller's "Arachnologies" (a term she opposes to Barthes's "hyphologies"):

> [W]hen a theory of the text called "hyphology" chooses the spider's *web* over the spider, and the concept of textuality called the "writerly" chooses the threads of lace over the lacemaker (*S/Z* 160), the productive agency of the subject is self-consciously erased by a model of text production which acts to foreclose the question of identity itself. (271)

Miller's reference to Barthes's *S/Z* is to the English translation (trans. Richard Howard, New York: Hill and Wang, 1975). Her reference in the French edition will be found on pages 165-66. Here Barthes begins his elaboration of the *texte veut dire tissu* motif:

> L'ensemble des codes, dès lors qu'ils sont pris dans le travail, dans la marche de la lecture, constitue une tresse (*texte, tissu* et *tresse*, c'est la même chose); chaque code, chaque fil est une voix; ces voix tressées— ou tressantes—forment l'écriture[.] (*S/Z* 166)

[8] Lucien Dällenbach, for example, thus embroiders on textiles as textual metaphors:

> Métaphore emblématique du texte qui, à travers elle, réactive son étymologie, celle du *tissu* est évidemment privilégiée. Si elle constitue un véritable *topos* [...] elle le doit au fait que le texte partage avec le textile la propriété d'être un entrelacement—d'où les termes de *trames, tresse* ou *tissage* qu'on lui applique fréquemment—et par là même de constituer une *texture*, c'est-à-dire un arrangement réciproque d'éléments, un réseau relationnel ou, si l'on préfére, une *structure*. (125; Dällenbach's emphasis)

Chapter 1: "Hiéroglyphes tout purs": Representations of Writing

[1] Like Soriano, I am proceeding from Michel Foucault's germinal study on madness and civilization:

> The classical period—from Willis to Pinel, from the frenzies of Racine's Oreste to Sade's Juliette and the Quinta del Sordo of Goya—covers precisely

that epoch in which the exchange between madness and reason modifies its language, and in a radical manner. (Foucault, *Madness* xi-xii)

[2] Julia Kristeva's introduction to linguistics in Chapter 3, "La Matérialité du langage" (*Le Langage* 23-46), provides a clear and concise discussion of what is at issue in this chapter.

[3] The clearest exposition of this model remains Jakobson's own in "Linguistique et poétique" (*Essais* 209-48). Of course my purpose here is not to dispute, refine upon, nor incorporate the refinements of others into Jakobson's model, but simply to show that the two moments of this fable meet the formal requirements for an act of communication.

[4] For complementary details on the relation between literature and hieroglyphics in the Renaissance and seventeenth century, see Marc Fumaroli's recent "Hiéroglyphes et lettres" in an issue of *Dix-septième Siècle* devoted to hieroglyphics.

[5] Quoted in Couton, "Réapprendre" 83. The title page of Ripa's 1603 Rome edition (actually the third edition but the first to include the woodcuts to which Baudoin refers) makes no mention of hieroglyphics.

[6] See Bassy, especially Chapters 1-2, for an interesting study of the place of emblems and book illustrations in the visual culture of La Fontaine's time.

Chapter 2: Book, Brain, Body:
Citation and the Scene of Reading:

[1] Genette has shown (*Figures II*, "Vraisemblance et motivation") to what extent this "natural attitude of society" was in the seventeenth century linked to the existence of a maxim. I will take up this problem later on in this chapter. The problem will come up again in Chapter 4 on "Les Deux Pigeons," in which the arguments of the two pigeons turn on contradictory maxims.

[2] J. Hillis Miller usefully reminds us of the slippery nature of many of our concepts in *para-*:

> "Para" is a double antithetical prefix signifying at once proximity and distance, similarity and difference, interiority and exteriority, something inside a domestic economy and at the same time outside it, something this side of a boundary line, threshold, or margin, and also beyond it, equivalent in status and also secondary or subsidiary, submissive, as of guest to host, slave to master. (219)

[3] I would like to note in passing that the falseness of the people's ideas is represented in this fable by an optical metaphor ("Mettant de faux milieux entre la chose et lui"), which Chamfort likens to a veil: "[. . .] une idée fausse qui nous empêche de porter sur une chose un jugement sain, est comme un voile interposé entre nous et l'objet que nous voulons juger" (Chamfort 142; qtd. in ed. Régnier 2: 341). I will examine the strategy of the veil, optical metaphors, and their relation to textuality in more detail in Chapter 7.

[4] It is probably entirely a coincidence that this scene takes place in an explicit scene of reading (Jesus reading in the synagogue), the only clear reference in the Scriptures that Jesus knew how to read (R. Brown, *Jerome Biblical Commentary* 2: 131).

[5] For a point by point comparison of La Fontaine's philosophy with that of his friend Bernier, see Jasinski, "Sur la philosophie de La Fontaine." Jasinski's study remains the best available on this important point. His conclusions are undeniable: La Fontaine was heavily influenced by Gassendi's Neo-Epicureanism. Jasinski concludes, citing the verses from "Démocrite," that the fables "prêchent la recherche scientifique et philosophique" (234). See also Couton, "Le Livre épicurien," in which Couton reads Book 8 of the *Fables* as an extended meditation on Epicureanism.

[6] According to Régnier, La Fontaine's most probable source was Bompart's seventeenth-century translation *Conférences d'Hippocrate et de Démocrite, traduites du grec en français, avec un commentaire* (1632). This important document in medical history has been recently translated and annotated by Yves Hersant. The last edition previous to this one was Emile Littré's 1861 edition.

See Jean Starobinski's "Démocrite parle" for his analysis of the role of Democritus and Hippocrates in Robert Burton's *Anatomy of Melancholy* (1628). Starobinski also recapitulates the literary history of the Democritus-Hippocrates couple in Erasmus, Montaigne, La Bruyère, Fénelon, and Samuel Beckett.

Here, and where appropriate in subsequent chapters, I will adopt the convention of designating La Fontaine's characters by their French spelling while reserving the conventional English spelling for other contexts in which the proper name might occur.

[7] One cannot, however, deny this structure's appeal. Biard himself inadvertently demonstrates its deceptive power. In order to emphasize this forceful series of binary oppositions, he typographically dislocates the verses in question:

> [. . .] Hippocrate arriva dans le temps
>   n'avoir raison
> Que celui qu'on disait
>   ni sens

```
                    dans l'homme
Cherchait
                    et dans la bête
                                        soit le cœur
Quel siège a la raison
                                        soit l'esprit.
```
(209)

Notice that the word *esprit* has been substituted for the word *tête*, producing, it is true, a more "normal" semantic opposition, but not the one in La Fontaine's verse. I would suggest that the power of the semantic oppositions, the strength of the structure itself, has caused this careful and perspicacious critic to misread and miscopy these verses. The same significant error occurs in Biard's original English version (150).

[8] I am here closely following Michael Riffaterre's account of readers' perception of intertextuality, a concept which he has rigorously elaborated in several germinal books and articles.

[9] See note 6 above.

[10] For an extended review of the concept of naturalization and its place in critical theory, see "Convention and Naturalization" in Culler, *Structuralist Poetics* 131-60. I will be using the term primarily to mean a fiction invented by the reader, a strategy to reduce surface strangeness by bringing the text, its anomalies, and incongruities into line with *doxa*.

[11] "Démocrite" contains the only explicit use of the word *labyrinthe* in the *Fables*. La Fontaine makes quite another use of the word in "La Chose impossible" (*Contes* 4.15).

[12] The lexical problem posed by the *doublets cerveau/cervelle* is of interest here. The former signifies the human brain and has few, but well attested, extended uses; the latter, properly an animal brain, has many figurative applications to humans.

[13] In "Sunken Images: Baroque Assimilation" (*The Brazen Tower* 93-119), Lapp demonstrates the importance of classical mythological imagery for the baroque poets despite the fact that mythological imagery is used "[. . .] discreetly, often almost imperceptibly, sometimes subsisting only in the names of characters" (93). He shows, too, the importance of disinterring these sunken images: "Close study may reveal, however, subtle differences in tone, subject, and emphasis, and in particular the way the myths are assimilated; how, in a manner of speaking, they go underground" (93). The second part of this essay treats sunken mythological images in La Fontaine's second "Discours à Madame de la Sablière."

[14] The mythology of the brain is particularly well developed in our own times. See "Le Cerveau d'Einstein" in Barthes, *Mythologies* 91-93. Perhaps it is no coincidence that Descartes's skull is conserved in the Muséum d'Histoire Naturelle in Paris and that the Didier school edition of the *Discours* (7) chooses to print a photograph of it.

[15] Gisèle Mathieu-Castellani, in her brilliant study of Renaissance anatomical engravings and their restructuring of the Renaissance notion of the body and death, makes a similar point: "L'anatomie est leçon, non seulement médicale et chirurgicale, mais éthique et métaphysique [. . .]" ("La Leçon d'anatomie," *Emblèmes de la mort* 126).

[16] Barker (78-79): "Despite the dense 'realism' perennially attributed to the painting's semiotic mode, it is already profoundly unrealistic in content in so far as no anatomy of the period ever began with the dissection of the hand [.]"

[17] See Barbara Herrnstein Smith's indispensable study of poetic closure as well as Richard Danner's *Patterns of Irony* (64-95), in which he relates closural to ironic effects in the *Fables*.

[18] La Fontaine and Chamfort, although mistaken, are at least in good company. Gallacher (13) thus quotes Pope Sylvester II: "Scriptoria dicente vox populi vox dei [. . .]."

[19] I am sure that some commentator must have pointed out the similarity of this passage with the Aesopic fable "Les Grenouilles qui demandent un roi" (*Fables* 3.4):

> Les Grenouilles, se lassant
> De l'état Démocratique,
> Par leurs clameurs firent tant
> Que Jupin les soumit au pouvoir Monarchique.

[20] Consider also Pierre Charron's quotation and acerbic revision of this adage quoted by Boas:

> Le vulgaire est une beste sauvage [. . .]. [L]a turbe populaire est mère d'ignorance, injustice, inconstance, idolatre de vanité, à laquelle vouloir plaire ce n'est jamais fait: c'est son mot, *vox populi, vox Dei*, mais il faut dire *vox populi, vox stultorum*. [. . .] (*De la sagesse* [1601], Book I, ch. 52; qtd. in Boas 31)

[21] For the modern reader, this proverb with all it presupposes has become hopelessly embroiled in an infernal logical labyrinth, since Flaubert quoted it, with Chamfort's para-doxal echo, as epigraph to his *Dictionnaire des idées reçues*: "Il y a à parier que toute idée publique, toute convention reçue, est une sottise, car elle a convenu au plus grand nombre." See Prendergast for one route through this labyrinth.

Chapter 3: Bodies and Souls: The Intertextual Corpus

[1] Geoffrey Bennington has noted La Fontaine's pre-Derridean "supplément":

> As in Derrida's use of the word *supplément*, the maxim indeed supplements the fable in both senses of the term: it is the additional element which comes to 'fill up' a lack in the narrative and complete the fable, and yet it remains an addition which the reader may have to 'supply' from outside. (*Sententiousness* 85)

[2] The bibliography of work devoted to this aspect of La Fontaine's *Fables* is too extensive to cite here. Two recent studies, however, provide a certain perspective on the problem as it pertains to our concerns in this chapter. Margaret McGowan rigorously applies this definition in her reappraisal of the essential role of the *moralité* in the fable genre in order to correct what she finds to be an abusive, modern tendency to emphasize the story at the expense of the moral. On the other hand, Marcel Gutwirth prudently reminds us that La Fontaine's too, too serious preface might well be all a part of the game: "Or celui qui dans la préface de son premier recueil donne gravement la moralité pour l'*âme* de l'apologue, dont la fable serait le *corps* (il cite là-dessus Aristote), et qui n'a rien de plus pressé, à la toute première de ses fables, que d'en faire sauter la morale—celui-là nous met suffisamment en garde contre une lecture simpliste" (159). La Fontaine does not, pace Gutwirth, cite Aristotle on the body/soul metaphor, but on whether plants and animals may be characters in fables. Aristotle himself has nothing to say on either of these points (ed. Couton, *Fables* 407).

[3] The history of this peculiar textual metaphor does not end with the classical era. Here, for example, is Jean-Paul Sartre's reflection on his childhood reading of the *Grand Larousse*: "Hommes et bêtes étaient là, en personne: les gravures, c'étaient leurs corps, le texte, c'était leur âme, leur essence singulière" (*Les Mots* 38).

[4] "Un Animal dans la lune" (*Fables* 7.17), the closing fable in Book 7, is another.

[5] Couton quotes (*Fables* 472) the most direct source for this tale in Bonaventure Des Périers's *Nouvelle XIV: Comparaison des alquemistes à la bonne femme qui portait une potée de lait au marché*. See as well Danielle Trudeau's study of the intertextual relations in the various avatars of this tale in Des Périers, Rabelais, and La Fontaine.

[6] Eleven days after reporting the strange death of M. de Boufflers, Mme de Sévigné sends her daughter a copy of La Fontaine's fable with this note:

> Voilà une petite fable de La Fontaine, qu'il a faite sur l'aventure de M. de Boufflers, qui fut tué tout raide en carrosse auprès de lui; cette aventure est

bizarre. La fable est jolie, mais ce n'est rien au prix de celles qui suivront. Je ne sais pas ce que c'est que ce *Pot au lait*. (*Correspondance* 1: 455)

This "farce" may not have a text, but it does have a title cited as well by Rabelais (*Gargantua* ch. 33). See ed. Couton (*Fables* 473) for other solutions to the mystery of the missing farce.

[7] Barthes (*S/Z* 27): "Ce qu'on appelle *code*, ici, n'est pas une liste, un paradigme qu'il faille à tout prix reconstituer. Le code est une perspective de citations, un mirage de structures."

[8] Trudeau (303): "[. . .] de même que la tête est à la fois objet visible et désignation de la faculté de penser, de même le pot au lait est à la fois objet porté et objet pensé, donc hors de la tête, mais aussi dans la tête."

Benveniste (295-96) shows that *testa* was used in late Latin as the medical term for the skull. The joke inscribed in the etymology of *tête* is not quite so funny anymore.

[9] While Furetière seems more interested in the social significance of *cotillon* ("on le dit particulièrement de celles des enfans, des paysannes, ou des petites gens"), the *Dictionnaire de Trévoux* (1752) attests the expression *aimer le cotillon*. "Joconde" (*Contes* 1.1) shows the erotic as well as the social connotations of *cotillon*:

> Sous les cotillons des grisettes
> Peut loger autant de beauté
> Que sous les jupes des coquettes.

[10] I would like to retain for the moment both the Pléiade's reading "Gros-Jean" as well as Couton's (and Régnier's) "gros Jean" for reasons that will become apparent further on.

[11] In Mme de Sévigné's account, it is the reverse. The deceased nobleman still retains his name, toponym of his estate, also mentioned by Mme de Sévigné, while the unhappy curé remains anonymous.

[12] For other functions of proper names in the *Fables*, see my "Naming Names."

[13] Furetière (*flatter*) quotes Nicod's etymology to this effect: "[. . .] il vient de *flatare* fréquentatif de *flo*, parce que les flatteurs soufflent toujours quelque chose aux oreilles de ceux qui les veulent ouïr." In La Fontaine's verse, *flatteuse* [*erreur*] is used in its classical sense as that which gives false hope. Racine is not above playing on this false etymology when he has Agamemnon evoke the Greek fleet's false start on its way to Troy: "Le vent qui nous flattait nous laissa dans le port" (*Iphigénie* 1.1.48).

[14] See Barbara Woshinsky's fascinating study of Corneille's exasperating use of metonymy, "'Aimer un bras': Metonymic Mutilation in Corneille's *Horace*."

La Fontaine's "Les Diadèmes vont sur ma tête pleuvant" is certainly no more or less burlesque than Corneille's "Trois sceptres à son trône attachés par mon bras / Parleront au lieu d'elle, et ne se tairont pas" (*Nicomède* 1.2.105-06).

[15] Régnier notes that *gros Jean* is "un homme de village ou d'humble condition" (2: 154) similar to *Gros Ian* or *Grand Tibault* in a *chanson paillarde* cited by Rabelais in his prologue to the fourth book (ed. Jourda 2: 22).

Chapter 4: Making the Difference: Textuality and Sexuality

An earlier version of this chapter was published as "Fragmented Lovers' Discourse: Textuality and Sexuality in La Fontaine's 'Les Deux Pigeons'" (*Papers on French Seventeenth-Century Literature* 9.17 [1982]: 675-90). I would like to thank editor Wolfgang Leiner for permission to use this material.

[1] For a selection of commentaries on this fable from the seventeenth through the nineteenth centuries, see ed. Régnier, 2: 358-68. Leo Spitzer ("L'Art de la transition chez La Fontaine") is the first of the modern critics to deal substantively with the anomaly of gender in "Les Deux Pigeons." In a later and lesser known article, "Nota sulla favola di La Fontaine: 'Les Deux Pigeons,'" he substantially modifies the theory of transitions he uses to resolve the "problem" of "Les Deux Pigeons." John Lapp analyzes this fable as a point of departure for his study of the *Contes* in *The Esthetics of Negligence*. See also Gutwirth (127-30) for a recent reappraisal of this fable.

[2] Gérard Genette devotes a chapter entitled "Le Genre de la rêverie" in his *Mimologiques* to the history of sexualizing metaphors from grammatical gender.

[3] This is true even if one concludes too hastily, I think, with Régnier that "il s'agit d'amitié, non d'amour au sens ordinaire" (2: 361n) or with Emile Faguet that La Fontaine "oublie qu'il a parlé de frères et il s'adresse aux amants" (qtd. by Spitzer, "L'Art de la transition" 186).

[4] See Genette, "Vraisemblance et motivation" (*Figures II*), for the function of maxims in the seventeenth century. See also Chapter 2 above for the functioning of contradictory quotations in the fable and the sense in which a maxim is in some senses a citation.

[5] Marc Fumaroli hears another voice, the voice of the psalmist, whom he quotes in Le Maistre de Sacy's translation:

> Et j'ai dit:
> Qui me donnera des ailes comme à la colombe,
> Afin que je puisse m'envoler, et me reposer?

> Je me suis éloigné par la fuite,
> Et j'ai demeuré dans la solitude.
> J'attendais là celui qui m'a sauvé de l'abattement
> Et de la crainte de mon esprit, et de la tempête.
> Précipitez-les, Seigneur,
> Divisez leurs langues,
> Parce que j'ai vu la ville toute pleine d'iniquité
> Et de contradiction.
> (Psalms 49 [or 50]. 6-9; trans. Le Maistre de Sacy
> [1665], qtd. in ed. Fumaroli, *Fables* 2: 360)

[6] H. Gaston Hall has proposed that "raven" is the only ornithologically correct translation of *corbeau*, usually translated "crow" to agree with the English language Aesopic tradition. His point (21) that "bird watching" may help prevent "word botching" is well taken.

[7] Marc Fumaroli sees much more going on in this passage:

> Est-ce forcer le sens de cette fable que d'y voir un résumé de toute l'entreprise poétique et sapientiale des *Fables*? [. . .] Les épreuves du pigeon conduisent celles que le lecteur a déjà faites au cours de cette odyssée fictive qu'a été déjà la lecture de *Fables*. L'orage (v. 33): *Le Chêne et le Roseau*. Le piège (v. 44-49): *Les Vautours et les Pigeons*. La fronde (v. 56): *L'Oiseau blessé d'une flèche*. Autant d'hiéroglyphes déjà rencontrés des périls qui menacent l'*homo viator*. (ed. Fumaroli, *Fables* 2: 360)

[8] For a discussion of traps and the *récit* as a trap in texts by La Fontaine, Retz, Perrault, and Racine, see Louis Marin, *Le Récit est un piège*. For a discussion of traps for unwary readers in La Fontaine's "Le Rat et l'Huître" (*Fables* 8.9), see my "Transtextual Traps."

[9] "[L]a syllepse consiste à prendre un même mot dans deux sens différents à la fois, sa *signification contextuelle* et sa *signification intertextuelle*" (Riffaterre, "La Syllepse" 496).

[10] See, for example, in Racine: "divins appas" (*Théb.* 2.1.329), "funestes appas" (*Mith.* 2.6.681), "invincibles appas" (*Brit.* 4.2.1169).

As a conventional image for feminine wiles, *las* may retrospectively be seen to be a part of the game. La Fontaine's fable evokes the cliché without the misogyny of its use in Ecclesiastes 7.27: "Et inveni amariorem morte mulierem, quae laqueus venatorum est [. . .]."

[11] John Lapp (*The Esthetics of Negligence* 1-2) uses the term *consubstantiality* in a quite different way to indicate a certain relation between the writer (Montaigne,

Rabelais, and La Fontaine are his examples) and his work: "The writer assures us that he and his work are one."

[12] Régnier (2: 365n) summarizes the philological problem of the word *volatile*:

> L'Académie, qui n'indique pas le genre de ce mot dans sa 1re édition (1694) et le fait masculin dans toutes les suivantes, dit, dans sa dernière seulement, qu'il "est aussi quelquefois féminin." Richelet (1679) ne donne que *volatille*, par deux *l*, qu'il qualifie de "mot burlesque" signifiant "tout animal qui vole," tandis que l'Académie, qui, dans toutes ses éditions a aussi cette forme en *ille*, conjointement avec l'autre en *ile*, entend la première seule des "oiseaux bons à manger."

CHAPTER 5: INSCRIBING THE VOICE:
ORAL PERFORMANCE AND THE WRITTEN TEXT

An earlier and considerably shorter version of this essay appeared as "Voice and Text: Representations of Reading in La Fontaine's *Psyché*" (*French Review* 52.2 [Dec. 1983]: 179-86). I am grateful to Ronald Tobin, editor of the *French Review*, for permission to use this material.

[1] Régnier, with characteristic completeness, cites classical, medieval, Renaissance and seventeenth-century occurrences of the Psyché and Cupid legend (8: 1-13). Thomas H. Brown's study is a useful complement to Régnier on the question of La Fontaine's sources. Apuleius's allegorical novel *The Golden Ass* is, of course, La Fontaine's most direct source for the Psyché story itself.

Anthony Blunt notes the importance of Francesco Colonna's *Hypnerotomachia Poliphili* (1499; French trans. *Le Songe de Poliphile*, 1543), cited by La Fontaine in the *avertissement* to *Le Songe de Vaux* (*OD* 79). Parallels between the Psyché story and the *Hypnerotomachia*, in which Poliphile searches for knowledge and a woman to love, are not limited to the plot line and "Poliphile," the name of Colonna's protagonist and La Fontaine's author. The "Myrtis and Megano" episode, which I will treat in some detail in this chapter, recalls Poliphile's (the Poliphile of the *Hypnerotomachia*, that is) deciphering of inscriptions and hieroglyphics as clues in his search for Polia. For the extraordinary importance of this work in every aspect of Renaissance and baroque culture, see Blunt, and Emanuela Kretzulesco-Quaranta, who sees in the iconographical program of the Grotto of Tethys at Versailles a virtual paraphrase of the *Hypnerotomachia*.

Françoise Graziani Giacobbi sees in *Psyché* clear indications that La Fontaine's *Psyché* is the rewriting of Marino's *Adone* as well. Her conclusions on La Fontaine's poetic enterprise are similar to my own:

[...] il conviendra de définir l'entreprise de La Fontaine comme une tentative de superposition intratextuelle de différents niveaux culturels, à partir d'une interprétation de la fable moins en tant que mythe qu'en œuvre littéraire. (397)

[2] For the sense of negligence in an author's style, see John Lapp, *The Esthetics of Negligence* 31.

[3] Page references will be to the Pléiade edition, *Œuvres diverses* (ed. Clarac), designated by *OD* in my text.

[4] See Gross's translation of these names and collation with La Fontaine's description of the four friends ("Functions" 578).

[5] For a resumé of commentators' refusal to give *Psyché* allegorical status, see Thomas H. Brown, *La Fontaine and Cupid and Psyché Tradition* 92. To this list one might add Gross's "Of course his [La Fontaine's] version is not allegorical" ("Functions" 577).

[6] Compare, for example, Armande's typically hyperbolic dictum in *Les Femmes savantes* (IV. iii.1173-74):

> Au changement de vœux nulle horreur ne s'égale
> Et tout cœur infidèle est un monstre en morale.

[7] See Goyet for a critique of Michael Riffaterre's notion of intertextuality based on the classical theory of *imitatio*.

[8] See David Shaw's study of the elaborate, precise network of correspondences that link Part 1 and Part 2.

[9] *The Iliad of Homer* (trans. Richard Lattimore) 104, vv. 154-60:

> And these, as they saw Helen along the tower approaching, murmuring softly to each other uttered their winged words: "Surely there is no blame on Trojans and strong-greaved Achaians if for long time they suffer hardship for a woman like this one. Terrible is the likeness of her face to immortal goddesses. Still, though she be such, let her go away in the ships, lest she be left behind, a grief to us and our children."

[10] Vergil, for example, has his shepherd-poet Mopsus lament the fallen Daphnis by reading the poem Mopsus had previously carved on beech trees:

> Immo haec, in uiridi nuper quae cortice fagi
> carmina descripsi et modulans alterna notaui,
> experiar: [...].
>
> (*Eclogue* 5.13-15)

Shakespeare brings the motif to the Forest of Arden:

> O Rosalind! these trees shall be my books,
>   And in their barks my thoughts I'll character,
> That every eye, which in this forest looks,
>   Shall see thy virtue witness'd everywhere
> Run, run, Orlando: carve on every tree
> The fair, the chaste, and unexpressive she.
> (*As You Like It* 3.2)

In Forez, Céladon's verses carved on the trees keep his memory alive when all believe him dead (Urfé, *L'Astrée* 38).

La Fontaine finds occasion to use the convention to cross-purposes:

> Hispal haranguait de façon
> Qu'il aurait échauffé des marbres,
> Tandis qu'Alaciel, à l'aide d'un poinçon,
> Faisait semblant d'écrire sur les arbres.
> Mais l'Amour la faisait rêver
> A d'autres choses qu'à graver
> Des caractères sur l'écorce.
> ("La Fiancée du roi de Garbe," *Contes* 2.14)

Lee (*Names*) documents almost a hundred paintings from the Renaissance through the nineteenth century that employ this motif. Most of his examples are illustrations of the key scene in Ariosto's *Orlando Furioso* in which Angelica and Medoro engrave their initials on the trees. Lee also distinguishes a second, elegiac, tradition derived more directly from the Latins (Vergil, Ovid, Propertius) in which a solitary lover laments the absence of the beloved. La Fontaine's *Psyché*, of course, belongs to this tradition.

While this motif is almost as old as pastoral literature itself, for at least one commentator the intrusion of writing into the pastoral garden represents a fall from grace: "Nothing could be clearer evidence of the loss of purity and plain confusion which befell the pastoral soon after its foundation by Theocritus than this self-defeating attack upon the surface of trees" (Rosenmeyer 203).

[11] Compare Paul H. Fry's conclusions on the epitaph in the Romantic period:

> [The epitaph] is at the furthest extreme in manner and purpose from the vocality of the sublime; it is not the pursuit of the voice but the burial of the voice, a concession to the tomblike bar between signifier and

signified that leaves only the bar itself as theme and place of presentation. The epitaph is the gravesite of the sublime. (433)

[12] Vuilleumier's article on "La Rhétorique du monument" is one of the few consecrated to this phenomenon in seventeenth century France. See also John Sparrow's now classic essay entitled *Visible Words*.

The seventeenth century did not lack for writers or theoreticians of inscriptions. Ménestrier (again!) is the author of a detailed study on the rules for building funerary monuments in which an important part is dedicated to inscriptions. Vuilleumier notes the diversity in Ménestrier's catalog of genres of inscription: "le motto, la légende, le titulus (socle de la statue), le titre (à l'indicatif présent: "Louis franchit le Rhin"), l'épigramme (cursives), l'inscription à l'antique (majuscules), l'inscription arguta ou l'éloge, la longue inscription en prose (cursives), la citation (Virgile, Bible)" (308).

[13] See Pierre Malandain's account of La Fontaine's "inscription fables" and their relation to the intertextual functioning of the fable (61-67).

CHAPTER 6: DESCRIPTION, REPRESENTATION AND INTERPRETATION

[1] Eugenio Donato takes up just this problem in "The Writ of the Eye" (963-64):

> The problem of the figure in the arts—but also the figure of the arts—is always that of two languages, more exactly two idioms, each with a presumed myth of an ultimate referent that ground them, apparently independent, yet problematically related, each hopelessly struggling to establish a hierarchical supremacy.

[2] The most striking use of the *ut pictura poesis* formula in La Fontaine's day was probably the opening verses of Charles Alphonse Du Fresnoy's Neo-Latin verse treatise *De Arte Graphica* (1667), which stress the reversibility of the pictorial and the literary work of art:

> Ut pictura poesis erit; similisque poesi
> Sit pictura;
>
> (qtd. in W. G. Howard 41)

W. G. Howard gives an account of the influence of this work in the seventeenth and eighteenth centuries. The history of the misreadings of the Horatian formula in the Renaissance and seventeenth century is well-documented in Lee (*Ut Pictura Poesis*), W. G. Howard, and Praz. Erica Harth's *Ideology and Culture in Seventeenth-Century France* is essential for understanding the importance of the *ut pictura poesis* model in all aspects of seventeenth-century culture.

For a provocative essay on the role of the reader in seventeenth-century painting, see Louis Marin, "Toward a Theory of Reading in the Visual Arts: Poussin's *The Arcadian Shepherds*." For *Psyché*'s place in the classical tradition, see Joan DeJean's article entitled "La Fontaine's *Psyché*: The Reflecting Pool of Classicism."

[3] The tension between description and narration will be explored more fully in the next chapter.

[4] The Grotto of Tethys in which Poliphile reads the first part of his *Psyché* was destroyed in 1684 to make room for the north wing of the palace. The central sculptural group depicting Apollo and his serving maidens (Girardon and Regnaudin), which La Fontaine describes at length, still exists and can be seen (with some difficulty) in a setting designed for it by the eighteenth-century painter Hubert Robert. Félibien's description with eleven engravings gives a much better idea of what this grotto was in the seventeenth century. See also Néraudeau (194-206) for the importance of this grotto in the ideological and mythological program of Versailles. For a fascinating discussion of the significance of grottos in Western art and culture, see Susan Sontag's "Grottos: Caves of Mystery and Magic."

[5] Of course the opposite is also true. One intent of La Fontaine's work was to memorialize Versailles, to give it a past, a story it never had. Versailles as site was new in an almost American way. It needed a "past," which our classical authors were to create using fragments of classical mythology redeployed in the service of the Sun King. For the way this was accomplished, see Néraudeau's study on this point.

[6] Pierre Clarac notes in his edition of *Psyché* the existence of a first edition corrected most likely in the hand of La Fontaine, which thus emends this passage: "Tout ce qui devait arriver *se lisait* selon les temps et la suite des aventures" (*OD* 825; my emphasis). This emendation stresses the narrativity and readability of Cupid's palace as text.

[7] Michael Riffaterre, "Sémiotique de la description dans la poésie du dix-septième siècle" 93. For his analysis of the intertext of art and artifice in modern poetry, which seems particularly relevant to texts written within the *ut pictura poesis* representational system, see as well his "Intertextual Representation."

[8] Hagstrum defines *ekphrasis* as "that special quality of giving voice and language to the otherwise mute art object" (18n). This definition, while consistent with the etymology of the term and its use in classical antiquity, has been considerably broadened, notably by Murray Krieger and Marc Eli Blanchard. For the extraordinary role

of *ekphrasis* in seventeenth-century rhetoric, especially that of the Jesuits, see Fumaroli, *L'Age de l'éloquence* 678-80. The essential problem of how voice is "given" to a literary or visual text is treated more fully in the previous chapter on *Psyché*.

[9] Apparently an ingenious system of hydraulic organs ("ressorts que l'onde fait jouer" [*OD* 133]) reproduced bird songs and, I suppose, the flutes as well (*OD* 829). The text does not always, however, so carefully distinguish between mimetic excess (blushing statues) and referential accuracy (singing birds).

Chapter 7: Reading (through) the Veil

[1] As early as 1757 the Comte de Caylus quotes these verses in his *Tableaux tirés de l'Iliade*. Lessing certainly knew them through Caylus even if he does not quote them directly (Lessing 208-09n). Irving Babbitt even states that "Lessing has done little more than develop the lines of La Fontaine" (48). Rensselaer Lee, in his now classic study suitably entitled *Ut Pictura Poesis*, quotes La Fontaine approvingly as a precursor of Lessing (8-9).

[2] The *Nouveaux contes* are the fourth collection of verse tales published by La Fontaine. I follow the editorial tradition observed in Régnier's edition in referring to them as Book 4, although La Fontaine himself did not. All quotations are from the Couton edition, *Contes et nouvelles en vers*.

The number of editions attests to the popularity of the *Nouveaux contes*. The paucity of contemporary critical allusions would tend to indicate how important they were considered (Grisé 249).

[3] John Lapp and Fannie Scott Howard have also, in quite different ways, treated the relation of the pictorial to the verbal in "Le Tableau." See also Nicolich on *Le Songe de Vaux* and DeJean on *Psyché*.

Of course, descriptions of paintings, real and fictive, were much in vogue in the seventeenth century. Two prominent examples are Giambattista Marino's *La Galeria* (1619), which exercised considerable influence throughout the century (see Praz 6; Fumaroli, *L'Age de l'éloquence* 212; and Graziano Giacobbi for Marino's influence on La Fontaine), and Pierre Le Moyne's *Les Peintures Morales* (1643), which explicitly takes up the Hellenistic ekphrastic tradition in the service of religion (Fumaroli, *L'Age de l'éloquence* 381-91).

[4] Recent theoretical studies in the wake of Michel Foucault have inscribed this relationship within a more general epistemological system. In her *Ideology and Culture in Seventeenth-Century France*, Erica Harth broadens the range of uses to which the Horatian formula has been put in using it to name the essentially aristocratic representational system that she finds in crisis from within and without and whose

eventual demise was concurrent with the end of the *ancien régime* (24-25). The historical horizons for what Timothy Reiss has called the analytico-referential class of discourse are somewhat broader ("Galileo, Frege, and Freud symbolize the limits *a quo* and *ad quem* of analytico-referential discourse" [26]), but he chooses Galileo's telescope, a conceit relating the visual and the verbal, as emblem and symptom of the instauration of the new class of discourse.

⁵ According to the title pages of the first edition (1674) and two subsequent editions (1675), the *Nouveaux contes* were published in Mons by Gaspard Migeon (Montgrédien 117; 119). This Gaspard Migeon, or correctly *Migeod*, had also consented to allow the Port Royal New Testament (1664), in fact printed in Amsterdam by the Elzevier, to bear his imprint. The *Nouveaux contes* were most probably printed in Rouen under the eye of their author (Martin 754).

⁶ For the ideological ramifications of the clandestine book trade and the significance of edition format for the seventeenth-century reader, see Harth 184; 187 ff. Genette (*Seuils* 21-25) treats the history and importance of book format as *péritexte éditorial*.

⁷ The passages from which La Fontaine borrowed directly are quoted at length in the Régnier edition (5: 577-78; Aretino, trans. Stafford 30-35). For the fresco episode see Aretino, trans. Stafford 12-15.

⁸ The effect of the inversion of what would normally be taken for principal and accessory has not been lost on at least one commentator on this tale (F. S. Howard 23):

> The author so effectively engages the reader's attention in moral, technical, and esthetic considerations that he tends to forget the story he is reading. Indeed, these questions eclipse and actually become the plot: the reader is more interested in seeing how the "ears" will make the picture perceptible to the "eyes" than in discovering the outcome of the story.

⁹ F. S. Howard speculates (22) that La Fontaine may have been inspired by an illustrated edition of the *Ragionamenti*. This is not proved, nor would a referential solution solve the problem of reference in this tale. Nonetheless the actual practice of covering paintings with curtains is well-attested. Giulio Mancini in his *Considerazioni sulla pittura* offers excellent advice on how and where paintings ought to be displayed, provides us with evidence for the practice of covering paintings, and introduces some interesting alibis for the use to which such paintings might be put:

> le [pitture] lascive, come Veneri, Marte, tempi d'anno e donne ignude, nelle gallarie di giardini e camare terrene ritirate; le deità nelle camare più terrene, ma più commune, e le cose lascive affatto si metteranno

ne' luoghi ritirati, e, se fusse padre di fameglia, le terrà coperte, e solo alle volte scoprirle quando vi anderà con la consorte o persona confidente e non scrupulosa. (1: 143)

He goes on to consider the role of such pictures in producing handsome children.

The couple depicted in William Hogarth's series "Marriage à-la-mode" (1742-46) has not taken Mancini's advice. The second painting in the series, "Shortly after the Marriage," shows the fashionable couple's picture gallery. It contains a painting covered by curtains just far enough open to show a naked foot. The viewer can easily guess what kind of painting is concealed by the curtain.

The *locus classicus* for stories of veiled paintings must certainly be Pliny's account of the competition between Zeuxis and Parrhasius (*Natural History* Book 35.36 [ed. Rackham 9: 309-10]). Zeuxis's painted grapes were so lifelike that birds came to nibble at them. After this great homage to his art, he asked that the curtains covering Parrhasius's painting be drawn. The curtains were the painting; there was nothing beneath the veil. Zeuxis had fooled the birds, but Parrhasius had fooled Zeuxis, the artist.

[10] Furetière's definition of *honnête* clarifies a word whose meaning has evolved considerably: "ce qui mérite de l'estime, de la louange, à cause qu'il est raisonnable, selon les bonnes mœurs." For the relationship between "honnêteté" and sexuality in the seventeenth century, see Roger Duchêne's essay on this subject.

[11] Compare Patrick Dandrey's conclusions ("Stratégie" 833) on the double reader in *Psyché*, quoted in the introduction to this study.

[12] See Chapter 6, note 8, on *ekphrasis*.

[13] This is precisely the point on which Homer's *ekphrasis* of Achilles's shield was criticized by the "Moderns" (Lessing 98).

[14] The "Catullus" cited here is rather the unknown author of the *Priapea*, wrongly attributed to Catullus. They have been recently republished and translated by W. H. Parker. The verses to which the tale alludes are:

> Nimirum sapiunt, videntque magnam
> Matronae quoque mentulam libenter.
>
> (Epigram 8)

These are the verses Montaigne deforms to deprecate his own sexual adequacy ("Sur des vers de Virgile," ed. Rat 2: 317).

[15] The veil and its variants have a long and distinguished history as metalinguistic figure. Its origins are no doubt somewhere in Plato's cave. Paul (2 Cor. 3.12-18) writes that a veil covers the hearts of the unconverted, preventing them from understanding the Law. See Origen's commentary on this passage and

Gerald Bruns's analysis of the differences in figuration in classical antiquity and in modern hermeneutics (156).

In the Middle Ages, the figure of the veil was closely associated by etymology with Christian doctrinal revelation, sacramental theology, and eschatology, as Thomas Aquinas shows in the final stanza of his "Adoro te devote":

> Iesu, quem velatum nunc aspicio,
> quando fiet illud quod tam cupio,
> ut te revelata cernens facie
> visu sim beatus tuae gloriae?
>
> (ed. Raby 403-04)

> (Jesus, whom now I see veiled,
> When will happen what I so desire,
> That seeing you with your face unveiled,
> I may be blessed with the sight of your glory?)
>
> (my translation)

Montaigne stresses the paradoxical functioning of the veil in a way strikingly similar to La Fontaine's ("Sur des vers de Virgile," ed. Rat 2: 308).

For the history of the veil figure in premodern texts, see Freccero's commentary on the veil figure in Petrarch, and in Dante's "Sotto il velame de li versi strani" (*Inferno* 9. 63); Rigolot's study of "Le Voile d'Olive" in his *Poétique* (Du Bellay, *Olive* 41, 72, 61) in which *voile* takes on important poetic functions as an anagram of *Olive* (*Poétique* 148-51); and my reading of Pierre Le Moyne's "Actéon" in "*Ekphrasis.*"

Leo Steinberg has discovered in the religious painting of the Italian Renaissance a painterly discourse centering on the revelation (unveiling) of Christ's genitals. This explicit gesture to the sexuality of Christ, which according to Steinberg was painted but never uttered (23), was meant to signify Christ's complete humanity. See also Steinberg's Excursus 20, "'Swags of Gossamer about the Hips'" (147), for a brief history of veils in classical literature and Renaissance art, and his Excursus 31, "Bowlderism" (174), for the nether side of veiling strategies.

Michel Foucault interestingly uses the figure of the veil to trace the difference between Renaissance and classical discourse:

A l'âge classique, connaître et parler s'enchevêtrent dans la même trame: il s'agit pour le savoir et pour le langage, de donner à la représentation des signes par lesquels on puisse la dérouler selon un ordre nécessaire et visible. Quand il était énoncé, le savoir du XVIe siècle était un secret mais partagé. Quand il est caché, celui du XVIIe et du XVIIIe siècle est un discours au-dessus duquel on a ménagé un voile. (*Les Mots et les choses* 103)

The veil as textual metaphor also occurs in Roland Barthes's fable of the text cited in the introduction to this study.

Jacques Derrida's interest in veils and related textiles is well known. See the following note.

Some recent studies, too numerous to cite here, explore aspects of the veil figure in modern literature. See Brivic for an exemplary treatment of this figure in Joyces's *Ulysses*. See, too, the first part of Michel Serres's meditation on *Les Cinq Sens* entitled "Voiles."

[16] " [. . .] the *hymen* is neither confusion nor distinction, neither identity nor difference, neither consummation nor virginity, neither the veil nor the unveiling, neither the inside nor the outside [. . .]" (Derrida, *Positions* 43). See also "The Double Session" (*Dissemination*, especially 212-13) for Derrida's reading of *hymen* in Mallarmé's "Mimique."

[17] For the concurrent development of optics and theatrical modes of representation in the seventeenth century, see Françoise Siguret's *L'Œil surpris: Perception et représentation dans la première moitié du XVIIe siècle*.

[18] The second epigram of the *Priapea* is a likely source for La Fontaine's refusal to choose the Muses as his helpers:

> Ludens haec ego teste te, Priape
> horto carmina digna, non libello,
> scripsi non nimium laboriose
> nec Musas tamen, ut solent poetae,
> ad non virgineum iocum vocavi.

I believe this is the first time a direct connection between the text of the *Priapea* and "Le Tableau" has been proposed.

[19] La Fontaine attests his absolute admiration for Homer in his "Epître à Huet" (*OD* 646). This important document for understanding La Fontaine's taste in literature is commonly dated 1687, the date of its publication. Mongrédien proves (117) that in fact it dates from 1674, making it exactly contemporary with the *Nouveaux contes*.

[20] The "couleurs," which figure painting in La Fontaine's formulation, must also be understood as rhetorical ornaments. Barthes's analysis of rhetorical *colores* as veil figures seems pertinent to my argument:

> [L]es couleurs sont parfois mises "pour épargner à la pudeur l'embarras d'une exposition trop nue" (Quintilien); autrement dit, comme

euphémisme possible, la "couleur" indexe un tabou, celui de la "nudité" du langage: comme la rougeur qui empourpre un visage, la *couleur* expose le désir en en cachant l'objet: c'est la dialectique même du vêtement (*schéma* veut dire costume, *figura* apparence). ("L'Ancienne Rhétorique" 218)

As for the opposition between narration and description, according to Gérard Genette, it did not in fact enjoy a very active existence before the nineteenth century. This is due, he says, to the unequal status of the two types of literary representation. While it may be impossible to conceive of narration without description, the reverse is rather easy to imagine, since "description is quite naturally *ancilla narrationis*, the never-emancipated slave" (*Figures of Literary Discourse* 133-34). Blanchard takes up just those texts in which "description pits itself against narrativity" (2-4).

CONCLUSION

[1] See Foucault, *Sexuality* 21, quoted near the beginning of Chapter 7.

[2] François Rigolot brilliantly explored the poetics of the name for the French Renaissance; a study of seventeenth-century onomastics of similar range and power is needed.

[3] See Proust, "Remarques sur la disposition par livres des *Fables* de La Fontaine," for a comprehensive statement of the problem. See also these readings of the *Fables* by book: Book 2: Gutwirth, "'Notre Homère': Les Douze Livres," in *Un Merveilleux* 181-97; Book 6: Gross, "Order and Theme"; Book 7: Danner, "'Les Vautours et les Pigeons'"; Book 8: Couton, "Le Livre épicurien"; Book 10: Danner, "The Labyrinth Hypothesis"; Book 12: Wadsworth, "Le Douzième Livre."

[4] See Madeleine Defrenne's "Architectures classiques" for her stimulating reflections on this problem.

Works Cited

Aretino, Pietro. *The Ragionamenti.* Trans. Peter Stafford. London: Odyssey, 1970.
Babbitt, Irving. *The New Laokoön.* Boston: Houghton, 1910.
Barker, Francis. *The Tremulous Private Body.* London: Methuen, 1984.
Barthes, Roland. "L'Ancienne Rhétorique: Aide-mémoire." *Communications* 16 (1970): 172-229.
———. *Essais critiques.* Paris: Seuil, 1964.
———. *Mythologies.* Coll. Points. Paris: Seuil, 1957.
———. *Le Plaisir du texte.* Paris: Seuil, 1973.
———. *Roland Barthes.* Paris: Seuil, 1975.
———. *S/Z.* Coll. "Tel Quel." Paris: Seuil, 1970.
Bassy, Alain-Marie. *Les Fables de La Fontaine: Quatre siècles d'illustration.* Paris: Promodis, 1986.
Baudelaire, Charles. *Œuvres complètes.* Ed. Y.-G. Le Dantec. Ed. rev. Claude Pichois. Paris: Pléiade-Gallimard, 1961.
Baudoin, Jean. *Recueil d'emblèmes divers.* 2 vols. Paris: Villéry, 1638-39. Rpt. Hildesheim and New York: Georg Olms, 1977.
Bennington, Geoffrey P. "Réappropriations." *Poétique* 48 (1981): 495-512.
———. *Sententiousness and the Novel.* Cambridge: Cambridge UP, 1985.
Benveniste, Emile. *Problèmes de linguistique générale.* Paris: Gallimard, 1966.
Beugnot, Bernard. "Autour d'un texte: L'Ultime Leçon des *Fables.*" *Travaux de Linguistique et de Littérature* 13 (1975): 291-301.
———. "Le 'Démocrite de la cour' (1641): Curiosité ou découverte?" *PFSCL* 10.19 (1983): 533-51.
———. "Spécularités classiques." *Destins et enjeux du XVIIe siècle.* Ed. Yves-Marie Bercé, et al. Paris: PUF, 1985. 173-81.
Biard, Jean Dominique. *Le Style des Fables de La Fontaine.* Paris: Nizet, 1969.
———. *The Style of La Fontaine's Fables.* New York: Barnes, 1966.

Biblia Sacra iuxta vulgatam versionem. 3rd ed. 2 vols. Stuttgart: Deutsche Bibelgesellschaft, 1983.
Blanchard, Marc Eli. *Description: Sign, Self, Desire.* The Hague: Mouton, 1980.
Blunt, Anthony. "The 'Hypnerotomachia Poliphili' in Seventeenth-Century France." *Journal of the Warburg and Courtauld Institutes* 1 (1937-38): 117-37.
Boas, George. *Vox Populi: Essays in the History of an Idea.* Baltimore: Johns Hopkins UP, 1969.
Boccaccio, Giovanni. *The Decameron.* Trans. Mark Musa and Peter Bondenella. New York: New American Library, 1982.
Boileau, Nicolas. *Œuvres complètes.* Ed. Françoise Escal. Paris: Pléiade-Gallimard, 1966.
Brivic, Sheldon. "The Veil of Signs: Perception as Language in Joyce's *Ulysses.*" *Etudes Littéraires Françaises* 57 (1990): 737-55.
Brody, Jules. "La Fontaine, *Les Vautours et les pigeons* (VII, 8): An Intertextual Reading." In *Convergences: Rhetoric and Poetic in Seventeenth-Century France.* Ed. David Lee Rubin and Mary B. McKinley. Columbus: Ohio State UP, 1989. 143-60.
―――. "Irony in La Fontaine: From Message to Massage." *PFSCL* 11 (1979): 77-89.
Brown, Raymond E., S. S., et al. *The Jerome Biblical Commentary.* 2 vols. Englewood Cliffs, NJ: Prentice, 1968.
Brown, Thomas H. *La Fontaine and Cupid and Psyché Tradition.* Provo, UT: Brigham Young UP, 1968.
Brunot, Ferdinand. *Histoire de la langue française des origines à nos jours.* 13 vols. Paris: Armand Colin, 1966.
Bruns, Gerald L. "The Problem of Figuration in Antiquity." *Hermeneutics: Questions and Prospects.* Eds. Gary Shapiro and Alan Sica. Amherst: U of Massachusetts P, 1984. 147-64.
Buffière, Félix. *Les Mythes d'Homère et la pensée grecque.* Paris: Les Belles Lettres, 1956.
Calvino, Italo. *The Uses of Literature.* Trans. Patrick Creagh. New York: Harcourt, 1986.
Chamfort, Sébastien-Roch Nicolas. *Notes sur les Fables de La Fontaine. Œuvres complètes de Chamfort.* Ed. P. R. Auguis. Paris, 1824-25. Rpt. Genève: Slatkine, 1968. 1: 77-198.
Clarac, Pierre. "Variations de La Fontaine dans les six derniers livres des Fables." *Information Littéraire* (Jan.-Feb. 1951): 1-9.
Collinet, Jean-Pierre. "L'Art de lire selon La Fontaine." *Europe* 515 (1972): 90-98.

Works Cited

Collinet, Jean-Pierre. *La Fontaine en amont et en aval*. Histoire et Critique des Idées 11. Pisa: Editrice Libreria Goliardica; Paris: Nizet, 1988.

———. "La Matière et l'art du prologue dans les 'Contes' de La Fontaine." *Studi Francesi* 25.2 (1981): 219-37.

———. *Le Monde littéraire de La Fontaine*. Paris: PUF, 1970.

Colonna, Francesco. *Hypnerotomachia Poliphili*. Venice: Aldus Manutius, 1499. Rpt. New York and London: Garland, 1976.

Compagnon, Antoine. *La Seconde Main*. Paris: Seuil, 1979.

Corneille, Pierre. *Œuvres complètes*. Coll. l'Intégrale. Paris: Seuil, 1963.

Couton, Georges. "Le Livre épicurien des *Fables*: Essai de lecture du Livre VIII." *Travaux de Linguistique et de Littérature* 13.2 (1975): 283-90.

———. *La Poétique de La Fontaine*. Paris: PUF, 1957.

———. *La Politique de La Fontaine*. Paris: Les Belles Lettres, 1959.

———. "Réapprendre à lire: Deux des langages de l'allégorie au XVIIe siècle." *CAIEF* 28 (1976): 81-101.

———, ed. *Fables choisies mises en vers*. See La Fontaine.

———, ed. *Contes et nouvelles en vers*. See La Fontaine.

Cronk, Nicholas. "The Singular Voice: Monologism and French Classical Discourse." *Continuum* 1 (1989): 175-202.

Culler, Jonathan. *On Deconstruction: Theory and Criticism after Structuralism*. Ithaca: Cornell UP, 1982.

———. *The Pursuit of Signs: Semiotics, Literature, Deconstruction*. Ithaca: Cornell UP, 1981.

———. *Structuralist Poetics*. Ithaca: Cornell UP, 1975.

Curtius, Ernst Robert. *European Literature and the Latin Middle Ages*. Trans. Willard Trask. Bollingen Series 36. Princeton UP, 1973.

Dällenbach, Lucien. *Le Récit spéculaire: Essai sur la mise en abyme*. Coll. Poétique. Paris: Seuil, 1977.

Dandrey, Patrick. "La Fable double de l'*Horoscope*: Une Poétique implicite de La Fontaine." *Dix-septième Siècle* 124 (July-Sept. 1979): 277-86.

———. "Stratégie de lecture et 'annexion' du lecteur: La Préface des *Amours de Psyché* de La Fontaine." *PFSCL* 14.27 (1987): 831-39.

Danner, G. Richard. "La Fontaine's *Fables*, Book X: The Labyrinth Hypothesis." *L'Esprit Créateur* 21.4 (1981): 90-98.

———. *Patterns of Irony in the Fables of La Fontaine*. Athens: Ohio UP, 1985.

———. "'Les Vautours et les Pigeons' and Book VII of the *Fables*." *PFSCL* 14.26 (1987): 185-91.

David, Madeleine V. *Le Débat sur les écritures et l'hiéroglyphe au XVIIe et XVIIIe siècles*. Paris: SEVPEN, 1965.

Davidson, Hugh M. *Audience, Words and Art: Studies in Seventeenth-Century French Rhetoric.* Columbus: Ohio State UP, 1965.

Defrenne, Madeleine. "Architectures classiques." *Destins et enjeux du XVIIe siècle.* Ed. Yves-Marie Bercé et al. Paris: PUF, 1985. 183-90.

DeJean, Joan. "La Fontaine's *Psyché*: The Reflecting Pool of Classicism." *L'Esprit Créateur* 21.4 (Winter 1981): 99-109.

Derrida, Jacques. *De la grammatologie.* Paris: Minuit, 1967.

———. *Dissemination.* Trans. Barbara Johnson. Chicago: U of Chicago P, 1981.

———. *Positions.* Trans. Alan Bass. Chicago: U of Chicago P, 1981.

Descartes, René. *Œuvres philosophiques.* Ed. Ferdinand Alquié. 2 vols. Paris: Garnier, 1963.

Dictionnaire de Trévoux. 7 vols. Paris: La Compagnie des Libraires Associés, 1752.

Dieckmann, Liselotte. *Hieroglyphics: The History of a Literary Symbol.* St. Louis: Washington UP, 1970.

Diogenes Laertius. *Lives of Eminent Philosophers.* Trans. R. D. Hicks. 2 vols. The Loeb Classical Library. New York: Putnam's, 1925.

Donato, Eugenio. "The Writ of the Eye: Notes on the Relationship of Language to Vision in Critical Theory." *MLN* 99.4 (Sept. 1984): 959-78.

Duchêne, Roger. "Honnêteté et sexualité." *Destins et enjeux du XVIIe siècle.* Ed. Yves-Marie Bercé et al. Paris: PUF, 1985. 119-30.

Du Marsais, César. *Traité des tropes.* Paris: Le Nouveau Commerce, 1977.

Flaubert, Gustave. *Le Dictionnaire des idées reçues. Œuvres complètes.* 28 vols. Paris: Louis Conard, 1910-36. 6: 415-52.

Foucault, Michel. *The History of Sexuality.* Trans. Robert Hurley. New York: Random, 1978.

———. *Madness and Civilization: A History of Insanity in the Age of Reason.* Trans. Richard Howard. New York: Random, 1965.

———. *Les Mots et les choses.* Paris: NRF-Gallimard, 1966.

Freccero, John. "The Fig Tree and the Laurel: Petrarch's Poetics." *Diacritics* 5.1: 34-40.

Fry, Paul H. "The Absent Dead: Wordsworth, Byron, and the Epitaph." *Studies in Romanticism* 17 (Fall 1978): 413-34.

Fumaroli, Marc. *L'Age de l'éloquence: Rhétorique et "Res Literaria" de la Renaissance au seuil de l' époque classique.* Genève: Droz, 1980.

———. "Hiéroglyphes et lettres: La Sagesse mystérieuse des Anciens." *Dix-septième Siècle* 158.1 (Jan.-Mar. 1988): 7-20.

———, ed. *Fables.* See La Fontaine.

Works Cited

Furetière, Antoine. *Dictionnaire universel* ... 3 vols. 1690. Rpt. Genève: Slatkine, 1970.
Gallacher, S. A. "Vox Populi, Vox Dei." *Philological Quarterly* 24.1 (Jan. 1945): 12-19.
Gass, William H. *Habitations of the Word*. New York: Simon, 1985.
Gaucheron, Jacques. "Visage de La Fontaine à 350 ans." *Europe* 515 (Mar. 1972): 3-21.
Genette, Gérard. *Figures I*. Paris: Seuil, 1966.
―――. *Figures II*. Coll. "Tel Quel." Paris: Seuil, 1969.
―――. *Figures of Literary Discourse*. Trans. Alan Sheridan. New York: Columbia UP, 1982.
―――. *Mimologiques: Voyage en Cratylie*. Paris: Seuil, 1976.
―――. *Seuils*. Paris: Seuil, 1987.
Gide, André. *Voyage au Congo*. Paris: Gallimard, 1927.
Gohin, Ferdinand. *L'Art de La Fontaine dans ses Fables*. Paris: Garnier, 1929.
Goldberg, Jonathan. *Voice Terminal Echo: Postmodernism and English Renaissance Texts*. London: Methuen, 1986.
Goyet, Francis. "*Imitatio* ou intertextualité (Riffaterre Revisited)." *Poétique* 71 (Sept. 1987): 313-20.
Graziani Giacobbi, Françoise. "La Fontaine lecteur de Marino: *Les Amours de Psiché* [sic], œuvre hybride." *Revue de Littérature Comparée* 232.4 (1984): 389-97.
Grisé, Catherine. "Le Jeu de l'imitation: Un Aspect de la réception des *Contes* de La Fontaine." *PFSCL* 10.18 (1983): 249-62.
Gross, Nathan. "Functions of the Framework in La Fontaine's 'Psyché.'" *PMLA* 84 (1969): 577-86.
―――. "Order and Theme in La Fontaine's *Fables*, Book VI." *L'Esprit Créateur* 21.4 (1981): 78-89.
Gutwirth, Marcel. *Un Merveilleux sans éclat: La Fontaine ou la poésie exilée*. Histoire des Idées et Critique Littéraire 246. Genève: Droz, 1987.
Hagstrum, Jean H. *The Sister Arts*. Chicago: U of Chicago P, 1958.
Hall, H. Gaston. "On Birds in La Fontaine's Fables." *PFSCL* 12.22 (1985): 15-27.
Harth, Erica. *Ideology and Culture in Seventeenth-Century France*. Ithaca: Cornell UP, 1983.
Hepp, Noémi. *Homère en France au XVIIe siècle*. Paris: Klincksieck, 1968.
Herodotus. *The Persian Wars*. Trans. George Rawlison. *The Greek Historians*. 2 vols. New York: Random, 1942. 1: 3-563.
Hippocrate. *Sur le rire et la folie*. Préface, traduction et notes d'Yves Hersant. Coll. Petite Bibliothèque Rivages. Paris: Rivages, 1989.

Hirsch, E. D. "Counterfactuals in Interpretation." *Texte* 3 (1984): 15-28.
Homer. *The Iliad of Homer.* Trans. Richard Lattimore. Chicago: U of Chicago P, 1951.
Horace. *Opera.* Oxford: Clarendon, 1901.
Howard, Fannie Scott. "La Fontaine's 'Le Tableau': A Consideration of the Parallel of Poetry and Painting." *FLS* 2 (1975): 15-26.
Howard, William Guild. "Ut Pictura Poesis." *PMLA* 24 (1909): 40-123.
Jakobson, Roman. *Essais de linguistique générale.* Paris: Minuit, 1963.
Jasinski, René. "Sur la philosophie de La Fontaine dans les Livres VII XII des *Fables.*" *Revue des Sciences Humaines* 2 (July 1934): 218-42.
Jauss, Hans Robert. *Toward an Aesthetic of Reception.* Trans. Timothy Bahti. Theory and History of Literature 2. Minneapolis: U of Minnesota P, 1982.
Jehasse, Jean. "Démocrite et la Renaissance de la critique." *Etudes seiziémistes offertes à V. L. Saulnier.* Travaux d'Humanisme et de Renaissance 177. Genève: Droz, 1980. 41-64.
Judovitz, Dalia. "The Graphic Text: The Nude in *L'Astrée.*" *PFSCL* 15.29 (1988): 529-41.
Kretzulesco-Quaranta, Emanuela. *Les Jardins du songe: Poliphile et la mystique de la Renaissance.* Paris: Les Belles Lettres, 1976.
Krieger, Murray. "The Ekphrastic Principle and the Still Movement of Poetry: Or, Laokoön Revisited." *The Play and Place of Criticism.* Baltimore: Johns Hopkins UP, 1967. 105-28.
Kristeva, Julia. *Le Langage, cet inconnu: Une Invitation à la linguistique.* Coll. Points. Paris: Seuil, 1981.
La Fontaine, Jean de. *Contes et nouvelles en vers.* Ed. Georges Couton. Paris: Garnier, 1961.
———. *Fables.* Ed. Marc Fumaroli. 2 vols. Lettres Françaises. Paris: Imprimerie Nationale, 1985.
———. *Fables choisies mises en vers.* Ed. Georges Couton. Paris: Garnier, 1962.
———. *Œuvres complètes: Fables, contes et nouvelles.* Ed. E. Pilon, R. Groos, et J. Schiffrin. Paris: Pléiade-Gallimard, 1954.
———. *Œuvres de J. de La Fontaine.* Ed. Henri Régnier. 12 vols. Les Grands Ecrivains de la France. Paris: Hachette, 1883-92.
———. *Œuvres diverses.* Ed. Pierre Clarac. Paris: Pléiade-Gallimard, 1958.
Lapp, John C. *The Brazen Tower: Essays on Mythological Imagery in the French Renaissance and Baroque.* Stanford French and Italian Studies 7. Saratoga, CA: Anma Libri, 1977.
———. *The Esthetics of Negligence: La Fontaine's Contes.* Cambridge: Cambridge UP, 1971.

Works Cited

Lee, Rensselaer W. *Names on Trees: Ariosto into Art.* Princeton: Princeton UP, 1977.

———. *Ut Pictura Poesis: The Humanistic Theory of Painting.* New York: Norton, 1967.

Lessing, Gotthold Ephraim. *Laocoön: An Essay on the Limits of Painting and Poetry.* Trans. Edward Allen McCormick. Baltimore: Johns Hopkins UP, 1984.

Lévi-Strauss, Claude. *La Pensée sauvage.* Paris: Plon, 1962.

Littré, Emile. *Dictionnaire de la langue française.* Paris: Gallimard, Hachette, 1968.

Logan, Marie-Rose. "Texte, Textus, Hyphos." *L'Esprit Créateur* 22.1 (Spring 1982): 69-78.

Lyons, John D. "Author and Reader in the Fables." *French Review* 49 (1975): 59-67.

———. "Speaking in Pictures, Speaking of Pictures: Problems of Representation in the Seventeenth Century." *Mimesis—From Mirror to Method, Augustine to Descartes.* Ed. John D. Lyons and Stephen G. Nichols. Hanover, NH: UP of New England, 1982. 166-87.

Magné, B. "*La Laitière et le Pot au lait* ou les comptes de Perrette." *Cahiers de Littérature du XVIIe Siècle* 4 (1982): 67-89.

Malandain, Pierre. *La Fable et l'intertexte.* Coll. ENTAILLE/S. Paris: Temps Actuels, 1981.

Mancini, Giulio. *Considerazioni sulla pittura.* Ed. Adriana Marucchi. 2 vols. Roma: Accademia Nazionale dei Lincei, 1956.

Marin, Louis. *Le Récit est un piège.* Paris: Minuit, 1978.

———. "Le Récit originaire, l'origine du récit, le récit de l'origine." *PFSCL* 11 (Summer 1979): 13-28.

———. "Toward a Theory of Reading in the Visual Arts: Poussin's *The Arcadian Shepherds.*" *The Reader in the Text.* Ed. Susan R. Suleiman and Inge Crosman. Princeton: Princeton UP, 1980.

———. "La Voix d'un conte: Entre La Fontaine et Perrault, sa récriture." *Critique* 36: 333-42.

Martin, Henri-Jean. *Livre, pouvoirs et société à Paris au XVIIe siècle (1598-1701).* 2 vols. Genève: Droz, 1969.

Mathieu-Castellani, Gisèle. *Emblèmes de la mort: Le Dialogue de l'image et du texte.* Paris: Nizet, 1988.

Maurand, G. "La Laitière et le pot au lait: Analyse sémio-linguistique." *Actes du Colloque d'Albi: Langages et signification.* Toulouse: Université de Toulouse-Le Mirail, 1980. 6-49.

McGowan, Margaret M. "Moral Intention in the *Fables* of La Fontaine." *Journal of the Warburg and Courtauld Institute* 29 (1966): 264-82.

Merino-Morais, Jane. *Différence et répétition dans les "Contes" de La Fontaine.* U of Florida Monographs: Humanities 52. Gainesville: UP of Florida, 1981.
Meschonnic, Henri. *Pour la poétique.* Paris: Seuil, 1970.
Mesnard, Jean. "Pourquoi les *Pensées* de Pascal se présentent-elles sous forme de fragments?" *PFSCL* 10.19 (1983): 635-49.
Miller, J. Hillis. "The Critic as Host." *Deconstrution and Criticism.* Ed. Geoffrey Hartman. New York: Seabury, 1979. 217-53.
Miller, Nancy K. "Arachnologies: The Woman, the Text and the Critic." *The Poetics of Gender.* Ed. Nancy K. Miller. New York: Columbia UP, 1986. 270-95.
Molière. *Œuvres complètes.* Coll. l'Intégrale. Paris: Seuil, 1962.
Mongrédien, Georges. *Recueil des textes et des documents du XVIIe siècle relatifs à La Fontaine.* Paris: CNRS, 1973.
Montaigne, Michel de. *Essais.* Ed. Maurice Rat. 2 vols. Paris: Garnier, 1962.
Néraudeau, Jean-Pierre. *L'Olympe du roi-soleil: Mythologie et idéologie royale au Grand Siècle.* Coll. Nouveaux Confluents. Paris: "Les Belles Lettres," 1986.
Nicolich, Robert. "The Triumph of Language: The Sister Arts and Creative Activity in La Fontaine's *Songe de Vaux.*" *L'Esprit Créateur* 21.4 (Winter 1981): 10-21.
Ong, Walter J., S. J. "The Writer's Audience Is Always a Fiction." *Interfaces of the Word: Studies in the Evolution of Consciousness and Culture.* Ithaca and London: Cornell UP, 1977. 53-81.
Peyre, Henri. Rev. of *Patterns of Irony in the Fables of La Fontaine,* by Richard Danner. *French Review* 60.1 (Oct. 1986): 119-20.
Pliny. *Natural History.* Ed. H. Rackham. 10 vols. Loeb Classical Library. Cambridge: Harvard UP; London: Heinemann, 1952.
Praz, Mario. *Mnemosyne: The Parallel between Literature and the Visual Arts.* Bollingen Series 35. Princeton: Princeton UP, 1970.
Prendergast, Christopher. "Flaubert: Quotation, Stupidity and the Cretan Liar Paradox." *French Studies* 35.3 (July 1981): 261-77.
Priapea: Poems for a Phallic God. Trans. W. H. Parker. London: Croom Helm, 1988.
Proust, Jacques. "Remarques sur la disposition par livres des *Fables* de La Fontaine." *De Jean Lemaire de Belges à Jean Giraudoux: Mélanges offerts à Pierre Jourda.* Paris: Nizet, 1970.
Raby, F. J. E., ed. *Oxford Book of Mediaeval Latin Verse.* Oxford: Clarendon, 1966.
Racine, Jean. *Œuvres complètes.* Coll. l'Intégrale. Paris: Seuil, 1962.
Régnier, Henri, ed. *Œuvres de J. de La Fontaine.* See La Fontaine.

Works Cited

Reiss, Timothy J. *The Discourse of Modernism*. Ithaca: Cornell UP, 1982.
Riffaterre, Michael. "Intertextual Representation: On Mimesis as Interpretive Discourse." *Critical Inquiry* 11 (Sept. 1984): 141-62.
———. *Semiotics of Poetry*. Bloomington: Indiana UP, 1978.
———. "Sémiotique de la description dans la poésie du dix-septième siècle." *Actes de Fordham*. Ed. Jean Macary. Biblio 17, 9. Paris, Seattle, Tübingen: PFSCL, 1983. 91-124.
———. "La Syllepse intertextuelle." *Poétique* 40: 496-501
———. "Textuality: W. H. Auden's 'Musée de Beaux Arts.'" *Textual Analysis*. Ed. Mary Ann Caws. New York: MLA, 1986. 1-13.
Rigolot, François. *Poétique et onomastique: L'Example de la Renaissance*. Genève: Droz, 1977.
Ripa, Cesare. *Iconologia*. 3rd ed. Rome, 1603. Rpt. Hildesheim and New York: Georg Olms, 1970.
Rosenmeyer, Thomas G. *The Green Cabinet: Theocritus and the European Pastoral Lyric*. Berkeley: U of California P, 1969.
Rubin, David Lee. "Four Modes of Double Irony in La Fontaine's *Fables*." *The Equilibrium of Wit: Essays for Odette de Mourgues*. French Forum Monographs 36. Lexington: French Forum, 1982. 201-12.
Runte, Roseann. "Narrator and Reader: Keys to Irony in La Fontaine." *Australian Journal of French Studies* 16 (1979): 389-400.
Russell, Daniel S. *The Emblem and Device in France*. French Forum Monographs 59. Lexington: French Forum, 1985.
Sartre, Jean-Paul. *Les Mots*. Paris: NRF-Gallimard, 1964.
Serres, Michel. *Les Cinq Sens*. Paris: Grasset, 1985.
———. *Le Parasite*. Paris: Grasset, 1980.
Sévigné, Madame de. *Correspondance*. Ed. Roger Duchêne. 2 vols. Paris: Pléiade-Gallimard, 1972.
Shakespeare, William. *Complete Works*. Ed. W. J. Craig. London: Oxford UP, 1971.
Shaw, David. "L'Esthétique de la structure dans 'Psyché' de La Fontaine." *Studi Francesi* 49 (1973): 15-27.
Siguret, Françoise. *L'Œil surpris: Perception et représentation dans la première moitié du XVIIe siècle*. Biblio 17, 22. Paris, Seattle, Tübingen: PFSCL, 1985.
Smith, Barbara Herrnstein. *Poetic Closure: A Study of How Poems End*. Chicago: U of Chicago P, 1968.
Sontag, Susan. "Grottos: Caves of Mystery and Magic." *House and Garden* 155.2 (Feb. 1983): 96+.
Soriano, Marc. "Les Histoires de fous chez La Fontaine." *Stanford French Review* 1.1 (Spring 1977): 5-27.

Sparrow, John. *Visible Words: A Study of Inscriptions in and as Books and Works of Art.* London: Cambridge UP, 1969.
Spitzer, Leo. "L'Art de la transition chez La Fontaine." *Etudes de style.* Paris: Gallimard, 1970. 165-207.
———. "Nota sulla favola di La Fontaine 'Les Deux Pigeons.'" *Studi Francesi* 7 (1959): 86-88.
Starobinski, Jean. "Démocrite parle." *Le Débat* 29 (Mar. 1984): 49-72.
Steinberg, Leo. *The Sexuality of Christ in Renaissance Art and in Modern Oblivion.* New York: Pantheon, 1984.
Sweetser, Marie-Odile. *La Fontaine.* TWAS 788. Boston: G. K. Hall, 1987.
———. "Réflexions sur la Poétique de La Fontaine: Le Jeu des genres." *PFSCL* 14.27 (1987): 637-51.
Tesauro, Emanuele. *Il Cannochiale aristotelico.* 1670. Rpt. Bad Homburg: Gehlen, 1968.
Tiefenbrun, Susan W. "Signs of Irony in La Fontaine's *Fables.*" *PFSCL* 11 (1979): 51-77.
Trudeau, Danielle. "La Fortune d'un pot au lait." *Poétique* 71 (Sept. 1987): 291-312.
Urfé, Honoré d'. *L'Astrée.* Ed. Gérard Genette. Coll. 10/18. Paris: Union Générale d'Editions, 1964.
Valéry, Paul. *Œuvres* Ed. Jean Hytier. 2 vols. Paris: Pléiade-Gallimard, 1957.
Van Baelen, Jacqueline. "*Psyché*: Vers une esthétique de la liberté." *La Cohérence intérieure: Etudes sur la littérature française du XVIIe siècle.* Paris: J.-M. Place, 1977. 177-86.
Vergil. *Opera.* Ed. R. A. B. Mynors. Oxford: Clarendon, 1969.
Vincent, Michael. "*Ekphrasis* and the Poetics of the Veil: Le Moyne's 'Actéon' and La Fontaine's 'Le Tableau.'" *Continuum* (forthcoming).
———. "Fragmented Lovers' Discourse: Textuality and Sexuality in La Fontaine's 'Les Deux Pigeons.'" *PFSCL* 9.17 (1982): 675-90.
———. "Naming Names in La Fontaine's 'Le Chat, la Belette et le petit Lapin.'" *Romanic Review* 74.3 (May 1982): 292-301.
———. "Naming the Cid." *Pascal, Corneille, Désert, Retraite, Engagement: Actes de Tucson.* Eds. Jean-Jacques Demorest and Lise Leibacher-Ouvrard. Biblio 17, 21. Paris, Seattle, Tübingen: *PFSCL*, 1984. 179-87.
———. "Transtextual Traps: 'Le Rat et l'Huître.'" *PFSCL* 12.22 (1985): 39-57.
———. "Voice and Text: Representations of Reading in La Fontaine's *Psyché.*" *French Review* 57.2 (Dec. 1983): 179-86.
Voltaire. *Micromégas. Romans et contes.* Paris: Folio-Gallimard, 1972.

Vuilleumier, Florence. "La Rhétorique du monument." *Dix-septième Siècle* 156.3 (1987): 291-312.
Wadsworth, Philip A. "Le Douzième Livre des *Fables*." *CAIEF* 26 (1974): 103-15.
Woshinsky, Barbara. "'Aimer un bras': Metonymic Mutilation in Corneille's *Horace*." *PFSCL* 12.22 (1985): 238-46.
Youssef, Zobeidah. *La Poésie de l'eau dans les "Fables" de La Fontaine*. Biblio 17, 3. Paris: PFSCL, 1981.
Zoberman, Pierre. "Voir, savoir, parler: La Rhétorique et la vision au XVIIe et au début du XVIIIe siècles." *Dix-septième Siècle* 33.133 (1981): 409-28.
Zumthor, Paul. *Langue, texte, enigme*. Paris: Seuil, 1975.
———. *La Lettre et la voix: De la "littérature" médiévale*. Coll. "Poétique." Paris: Seuil, 1987.

Index

Fables and tales by La Fontaine are listed under his name under the appropriate category in alphabetical order with their book and poem number.

Abstemius, 18
Accident, 45-46, 52-53
Achilles's shield, 98, 106, 132n13
Adages, 23, 38-39. *See also* Proverbs; Maxims
Allegory, 16, 59, 60, 89, 105, 126n5. *See also* Reading: allegory of
Allusion, 6, 10, 21-23, 51, 72-73, 99
Ame. *See* Soul
Animals: animal code, 47; as characters, 48, 57; gender of, 56; as generic markers, 47; as money, 48; opposed to "human," 27, 29-30; as symbols, 56-57; thought in, 28-29
Anomaly, 6, 55-56, 59, 84
Antonomasia, 26, 93-94. *See also* Proper names
Apostrophe, 73
Apuleius, 69, 72; *The Golden Ass,* 125n1
Aretino, Pietro, 104; *Ragionamenti,* 93-94, 131n9
Ariosto, Ludovico, 127n10
Art des emblèmes, L'. See Ménestrier, Claude-François
Astrée, L', 62, 127n10
Author, 1, 7; authorial intention, 18, 20; of proverbs, 24
Authority, 37-39, 44, 99

Babbitt, Irving, 130n1
Barbin, Claude, 92
Barker, Francis, 34-35, 120n16
Barthes, Roland, 8-9, 23, 45-46, 116n7, 120n14, 122n7, 134n15, 134-35n20
Baudelaire, Charles, 102
Baudoin, Jean, 15-16
Bennington, Geoffrey, 23-24, 121n1
Benveniste, Emile, 115n4, 122n8
Beugnot, Bernard, 65, 110
Biard, Jean Dominique, 28-29, 118-19n7
Bible, 37-38; 2 Cor., 132n15; Eccles., 124n10; Luke, 24; Ps., 123-24n5; 1 Sam., 38. *See also* Intertext: biblical
Bienséances, 97-98, 105. See also *Decorum*
Binary opposition (pattern), 3-4, 23, 28-29, 118-19n7
Blanchard, Marc Eli, 97, 135n20
Blunt, Anthony, 125n1
Boas, George, 38
Boccaccio, Giovanni, 104; *Decameron,* 93-94
Body: disfigured, 61-62; of the emblem, 42; of the fable, 41-43; as hieroglyphic, 62; of Perrette as graphism (character), 49; and soul, 42, 121n2, 121n3; as textual metaphor, 42. *See also* Soul
Boileau, Nicolas, 92, 99

Brain (*cerveau*), 32, 34, 119n12, 120n14
Bricoleur, 19-20
Brody, Jules, 4, 6, 7, 9, 64
Brown, Thomas H., 126n5
Burlesque, 105-06

Calvino, Italo, 31
Cannochiale aristotelico, Il, 101
Catullus, 98-99, 132n14
Caylus, Anne Claude Philippe de Tubières, Comte de, 130n1
Censorship, 92-93, 98, 100
Cerveau. See Brain
Chamfort, Sébastien-Roch Nicolas, 37-38, 44, 60, 118n3, 120n18, 120n21
Champollion, Jean-François, 14, 110
Character: as inscription, 18; as proper name, 26-27
Charron, Pierre, 120n20
Citation, 10, 21-24, 35-36, 38-39, 57, 110
Clarac, Pierre, 129n6
Closure, 111-12, 120n17
Clothing, 49-51, 102
Code, 47-49, 122n7
Collinet, Jean-Pierre, 4, 5-6, 41, 43-46, 65, 95, 115n2
Colonna, Francesco: *Hypnerotomachia Poliphili*, 14, 69, 125n1
Communication theory, 3, 12-13, 117n3
Compagnon, Antoine, 20
Considerazioni sulla pittura, 131-32n9
Conte. See Tale
Corneille, Pierre, 38-39, 122-23n14
Corporeality, 34; corporeal code, 47, 49. See also Body
Corrozet, Gilles, 15-16
Couton, Georges, 16-17, 31-32, 42, 51, 111
Cronk, Nicholas, 110
Culler, Jonathan, 2, 31, 119n10

Dällenbach, Lucien, 116n8
Dandrey, Patrick, 4
Danner, G. Richard, 4, 31, 110-11, 115-16n6, 120n17
Dante Alighieri, 133n15
Davidson, Hugh M., 97

Decameron. See Boccaccio, Giovanni
Decorum, 97-98, 99. See also *Bienséances*
Deictics, 96, 103
Democritus, 28, 33, 118n6
Derrida, Jacques, 5, 13, 14, 42-43, 79, 100, 121n1, 134n15, 134n16
Descartes, René, 32, 39, 120n14; *Discours de la méthode*, 28-30, 34
Description, 81-82, 84, 88, 98, 107; opposed to narration, 107-08, 135n20
Des Périers, Bonaventure, 121n5
Deucalion, 72
Deus artifex, 99, 106
Dictionnaire de l'Académie, 16
Dictionnaire de Trévoux, 122n9
Dictionnaire universel.... See Furetière, Antoine
Dido, 58
Discours de la méthode. See Descartes, René
Displacement, 70, 73, 94-95, 98, 104
Dissection, 29, 32-34
Donato, Eugenio, 128n1
Doxa, 23-25, 30, 35, 39, 46, 119n10
Du Bellay, Joachim, 133n15
Duchêne, Roger, 45
Du Fresnoy, Charles Alphonse, 128n2
Du Marsais, César, 101-02

Ekphrasis, 88-89, 98, 99, 103, 106-07, 129-30n8
Emblems, 10, 12, 16-20, 42, 78; as *bricolage*, 19
Enzensberger, Hans Magnus, 31
Epicureanism, 24, 118n5
Epitaphs, 10, 76-77, 79, 127-28n11
Eros, 50; erotic code, 47, 49; erotic love, 60-61
Etymology, 2, 9, 33, 49, 52, 53, 63, 74, 98, 122n13

Fables: books of, 111-12, 135n3; double, 41-47; genre of, 41-42, 47, 56; interpretation of, 55; relationship to emblems, 16-17; as story, 55; structure of, 41

Faguet, Emile, 123n3
Fait divers, 43-46
Farce, 44, 46-47, 53, 122n6
Figurative expression, 32, 51-53
Flaubert, Gustave, 120n21
Folly (*folie*), 11-12, 13, 22, 25-26, 28, 48
Foucault, Michel, 92, 108, 116-17n1, 133-34n15
Fragonard, Jean Honoré, 50
Frame narrative, 65-66, 81-82, 84, 94, 96
Freccero, John, 133n15
Fry, Paul H., 127-28n11
Fumaroli, Marc, 64, 117n4, 123-24n5, 124n7
Furetière, Antoine, 32-33, 51, 122n9, 132n10

Gallacher, S. A., 38
Gaucheron, Jacques, 2
Gender, grammatical, 56, 63, 123n1, 123n2
Genette, Gérard, 19, 123n2, 123n4, 131n6, 135n20
Gide, André, 1, 6
Golden Ass, The. *See* Apuleius
Grammatology, 14
Graziani Giacobbi, Françoise, 125-26n1
Greimas, A. J., 115n1
Gross, Nathan, 67, 73, 82, 126n4, 126n5
Gutwirth, Marcel, 121n2

Hagstrum, Jean H., 103, 129n8
Harth, Erica, 96, 130-31n4
Hecatomgraphie, L', 15-16
Herodotus, 13
Hieroglyphica, 14
Hieroglyphics, 10, 12, 14-17, 20, 57, 62-63, 117n4
Hippocrates, 28, 33, 118n6
Hogarth, William, 132n9
Homer, 134n19; *Iliad*, 72-73, 98, 105-07, 126n9
Honnêteté, 132n10
Horace, 21, 24, 58, 81, 97
Horapollo, 14
Howard, Fannie Scott, 130n3, 131n8, 131n9

Hymen, 100
Hypnerotomachia Poliphili, 14, 69, 125n1
Hypotyposis, 101-02, 103

Iconologia, 15, 117n5
Imitatio, 71
Inscription, 10, 17-18, 42-43, 62, 74, 77-79, 128n12; Delphic, 25
Interpretation, 81; failure of, 69, 84-85
Intertext, 30; biblical, 24, 37-38 (*see also* Bible); Cartesian, 33 (*see also* Descartes, René); Rabelaisian, 51
Intertextuality, 7, 10, 34, 47, 58-59, 109, 110, 119n8
Irony, 3-4, 110; ironic reading, 25
Iser, Wolfgang, 4

Jakobson, Roman, 12, 117n3
Jasinski, René, 118n5
Jauss, Hans Robert, 4-5
Jesus (Christ), 24, 118n4, 133n15

Kretzulesco-Quaranta, Emanuela, 125n1
Kristeva, Julia, 117n2

Labyrinth, 10, 29, 31-33
La Fontaine, Jean de: *Les Amours de Psyché et de Cupidon*, 5, 14, 18, 65-80, 81-90, 94, 110, 112; "Epître à Huet," 134n19; "La Vie d'Esope le phrygien," 109
—*Fables*: "Un Animal dans la lune" (7.17), 101; "Les Animaux malades de la peste" (7.1), 47, 112-13; "L'Astrologue qui se laisse tomber dans un puits" (2.13), 19, 43; "Le Curé et le Mort" (7.10), 41-54; "Démocrite et les Abdéritains" (8.26), 21-40, 55, 112; "Les Deux Amis" (8.11), 60; "Deux Mulets" (1.4), 19; "Les Deux Pigeons" (9.2), 20, 55-64; "Discours à Madame de la Sablière" (9), 28; "Le Fou qui vend la sagesse" (9.8), 11-20, 22, 27; "Les Grenouilles qui demandent un roi" (3.4), 120n19; "Le Héron—La Fille" (7.4), 42, 49-50; "L'Homme et

La Fontaine, Jean de (*continued*)
son image" (1.11), 110; "Le Juge
Arbitre, l'Hospitalier et le Solitaire"
(12.29), 112; "Le Laboureur et ses
Enfants" (5.9), 7; "La Laitière et le Pot
au lait" (7.9), 41-54, 110; "Le Loup, la
Chèvre et le Chevreau"—"Le Loup, la
Mère et l'Enfant" (4.15-16), 78, 110;
"Les Obsèques de la Lionne" (8.14),
47; "Le Pâtre et le Lion" (6.1), 36; "Le
Pouvoir des Fables" (8.4), 109; Préface, 36, 41; "Le Rat et l'Huître" (8.9),
115n3; "La Souris métamorphosée en
fille" (9.7), 56; "Testament expliqué
par Esope" (2.20), 110; "Le Vieillard
et les Trois Jeunes Hommes" (11.8),
78-79, 110
—*Contes*: "La Fiancée du roi de Garbe"
(2.14), 127n10; "Joconde" (1.1),
122n9; "Mazet de Lamporechio"
(2.16), 93
—*Nouveaux contes*, 92-93, 95, 109, 130n2,
131n5, 134n19; "L'Abbesse" (4.2), 95;
"Le Cas de conscience" (4.4), 109;
"Les Lunettes" (4.12), 95; "Le Psautier" (4.7), 95, 109; "Le Tableau"
(4.17), 18, 91-108
Lapp, John C., 32, 119n13, 123n1, 124-25n11, 126n2, 130n3
Lee, Rensselaer W., 127n10, 130n1
Le Moyne, Pierre, 130n3
Lessing, Gotthold Ephraim, 130n1
Lévi-Strauss, Claude, 19
Literary code, 47
Littré, Emile, 61
Logan, Marie-Rose, 8
Lucretius, 112
Lyons, John D., 6

Malandain, Pierre, 7, 110
Mallarmé, Stéphane, 100
Mancini, Giulio, 131-32n9
Marin, Louis, 3, 109, 115n3
Marino, Giambattista, 125n1, 130n3
Marvelous, the (*le merveilleux*), 84
Mathieu-Castellani, Gisèle, 120n15

Maxims, 10, 23, 25, 35, 37, 57, 123n4
McGowan, Margaret M., 19, 121n2
Ménestrier, Claude-François, 16, 128n12;
L'Art des emblèmes, 19, 42
Merino-Morais, Jane, 115n1
Mesnard, Jean, 111
Metonymy, 27, 49, 122-23n14
Micromégas, 25
Miller, J. Hillis, 117n2
Miller, Nancy K., 116n7
Mimesis, 83, 89, 96, 98, 100
Molière [*pseud. of* Jean-Baptiste Poquelin],
126n6
Mongrédien, Georges, 134n19
Monster, 70-71, 86
Montaigne, Michel de, 132n14, 133n15
Moral: *morale*, 36; *moralité*, 36, 41, 47,
121n2

Narration: opposed to description, 107-08,
135n20
Naturalization, 30-34, 55-57, 63-64, 84, 90,
100, 102, 119n10
Novella (*nouvelle*), 96
Nudity, 105-06

Ong, Walter, 5
Onomastics: onomastic code, 47. *See also*
Proper names
Oracles, 66-67, 69-70, 86-87
Orality, 10, 66, 78
Oral performance, 66

Pantagruel, 51
Paradox, 23, 25, 27, 38-39, 45-46, 100,
117n2. *See also Doxa*
Paranarrative, 97, 104-05, 107-08
Parrhasius, 132n9
Pascal, Blaise, 101, 111
Periphrasis, 99
Petrarca, Francesco (Petrarch), 133n15
Peyre, Henri, 111
Pilpay, 57-58
Pliny, 132n9
Portraits, 87-88
Prediction, 59, 61

Index 153

Preface, 41, 97. *See also* Prologues, authorial
Prendergast, Christopher, 23
Presence, 83-84, 88, 94
Priapea, 132n14, 134n18
Priapus, 99-100, 106
Prologues, authorial, 94-97, 103
Proper names, 10, 26-27, 30, 36-37, 50-51, 53-54, 68-69, 110
Proverbs, 10, 21-24, 38-39; proverbial expressions, 48

Quotation. *See* Citation

Rabelais, François, 51
Racine, Jean, 122n13, 124n10
Ragionamenti. *See* Aretino, Pietro
Reader: double, 5; of emblems, 19-20; implied, 4-5, 37, 95-97, 100, 109; internal, 65, 74-75; as interpreter, 85, 90; of La Fontaine, 1-2, 7; in the text, 5-6. *See also* Reading; Naturalization
Reader reception, 2, 4-6, 10
Reading: allegorical, 69; allegory of, 59, 64, 97, 108; of emblems, 19-20; intertextual, 7; ironic, 70-71; pleasures of, 65; relation to madness (*folie*), 25-26; scenes of, 22, 30-31, 35, 68, 79, 85, 92, 109, 118n4
Récit, 36-37
Régnier, Henri, 35, 123n3, 125n12, 125n1
Reiss, Timothy J., 101, 131n4
Rembrandt van Rijn, 34
Representation, 83-84, 88, 96, 98, 108
Rhetorical question, 37
Riffaterre, Michael, 4, 7, 61, 67, 84, 119n8, 124n9, 129n7
Rigolot, François, 133n15, 135n2
Ripa, César, 15, 117n5
Rosenmeyer, Thomas G., 127n10
Rubin, David Lee, 3-4
Runte, Roseann, 44
Russell, Daniel S., 16, 19

Sartre, Jean-Paul, 121n3
Serres, Michel, 3

Sévigné, Marie de Rabutin-Chantal, Marquise de, 45-46, 121-22n6, 122n11
Sexuality, 92, 107-08, 133n15
Shakespeare, William, 127n10
Signature, 24, 53-54
Smith, Barbara Herrnstein, 112, 120n17
Society: social code, 47-48
Sophocles, 112
Soriano, Marc, 11-12
Soul (*âme*): and body, 18, 42-43, 64; as breath (*anima*), 52, 64. *See also* Body
Speech act, 13
Spitzer, Leo, 6, 58, 60, 63, 106, 123n1
Starobinski, Jean, 118n6
Steinberg, Leo, 133n15
Sweetser, Marie-Odile, 115n2
Syllepsis (*syllepse*), 13, 61, 124n9
Sylvester II (Pope), 120n18
Symmetry, 28-29, 30

Tale (*conte*): genre, 97, 102
Telescope, Galileo's, 101, 131n4
Tesauro, Emanuele, 101
Tethys, Grotto of, 82, 85, 89, 125n1, 129n4
Text: as textile (*tissu*), 9, 116n7, 116n8; figures of the text, 8-10, 109-10 (*see also* Writing); as veil, 9, 108 (*see also* Veil)
Textuality, 10, 39, 42-43, 111
"Theory," 2-3
Thomas Aquinas, 133n15
Tiefenbrun, Susan W., 3
Traps, 3, 59, 60-61, 86, 115n3, 124n8
Trudeau, Danielle, 121n5, 122n8

Ungrammaticality, 67
Urfé, Honoré d', 62, 127n10
Ut pictura poesis, 81-82, 88, 90, 91, 94, 96, 98, 104, 108,128-29n2

Valéry, Paul, 1
Van Baelen, Jacqueline, 66
Veil, 10, 50, 101-02, 108, 118n3, 132-34n15; veiled (curtained) paintings, 131-32n9. *See also* Clothing
Vergil, 58, 126n10
Versailles, 65, 82-86, 129n5

Vestimentary code, 47, 49. *See also* Clothing
Vision, 81, 101-03, 108
Voice, 57, 98; disembodied, 52-53; narratorial, 37, 104; opposed to text, 26, 66-67
Voltaire [*pseud. of* François-Marie Arouet], 25
Vox populi, vox dei, 21-22, 37-39
Vraisemblance, 35, 57, 83, 96, 98
Vuilleumier, Florence, 128n12

Woshinsky, Barbara, 122n14
Writing, 5, 42-43; of emblems, 19-20; as inscription, 74; opposed to speech, 12, 59, 65-66, 77, 79; pictorial, 18

Youssef, Zobeidah, 110

Zeuxis, 132n9
Zoberman, Pierre, 101
Zumthor, Paul, 66

Since its inception in 1980, PURDUE UNIVERSITY MONOGRAPHS IN ROMANCE LANGUAGES has acquired a distinguished reputation for its exacting standards and valuable contributions to Romance scholarship. The collection contains critical studies of literary or philological importance in the areas of Peninsular, Latin American, or French literature or language. Also included are occasional critical editions of important texts from these literatures. Among the authors are some of the finest of today's writers from both the new generation of scholars and the ranks of more established members of the profession. Writing in English, French, or Spanish, the authors address their subjects with insight and originality in books of approximately 200 pages. All volumes are printed on acid-free paper.

INQUIRIES CONCERNING THE SUBMISSION OF MANUSCRIPTS should be directed to the General Editor, Howard Mancing, Stanley Coulter Hall, Purdue University, West Lafayette, Indiana 47907 USA.

Available from
PURDUE UNIVERSITY MONOGRAPHS IN ROMANCE LANGUAGES

1. John R. Beverley: *Aspects of Góngora's "Soledades."* Amsterdam, 1980. xiv, 139 pp. Cloth.
2. Robert Francis Cook: *"Chanson d'Antioche," chanson de geste: Le Cycle de la Croisade est-il épique?* Amsterdam, 1980. viii, 107 pp. Cloth.
3. Sandy Petrey: *History in the Text: "Quatrevingt-Treize" and the French Revolution.* Amsterdam, 1980. viii, 129 pp. Cloth.
4. Walter Kasell: *Marcel Proust and the Strategy of Reading.* Amsterdam, 1980. x, 125 pp. Cloth.
5. Inés Azar: *Discurso retórico y mundo pastoral en la "Egloga segunda" de Garcilaso.* Amsterdam, 1981. x, 171 pp. Cloth.
6. Roy Armes: *The Films of Alain Robbe-Grillet.* Amsterdam, 1981. x, 216 pp. Cloth.
7. David M. Dougherty and Eugene B. Barnes, eds.: *Le "Galien" de Cheltenham.* Amsterdam, 1981. xxxvi, 203 pp. Cloth.
8. Ana Hernández del Castillo: *Keats, Poe, and the Shaping of Cortázar's Mythopoesis.* Amsterdam, 1981. xii, 135 pp. Cloth.
9. Carlos Albarracín-Sarmiento: *Estructura del "Martín Fierro."* Amsterdam, 1981. xx, 336 pp. Cloth.
10. C. George Peale et al., eds.: *Antigüedad y actualidad de Luis Vélez de Guevara: Estudios críticos.* Amsterdam, 1983. xii, 298 pp. Cloth.
11. David Jonathan Hildner: *Reason and the Passions in the "Comedias" of Calderón.* Amsterdam, 1982. xii, 119 pp. Cloth.
12. Floyd Merrell: *Pararealities: The Nature of Our Fictions and How We Know Them.* Amsterdam, 1983. xii, 170 pp. Cloth.
13. Richard E. Goodkin: *The Symbolist Home and the Tragic Home: Mallarmé and Oedipus.* Amsterdam, 1984. xvi, 203 pp. Paper.
14. Philip Walker: *"Germinal" and Zola's Philosophical and Religious Thought.* Amsterdam, 1984. xii, 157 pp. Paper.
15. Claire-Lise Tondeur: *Gustave Flaubert, critique: Thèmes et structures.* Amsterdam, 1984. xiv, 119 pp. Paper.
16. Carlos Feal: *En nombre de don Juan (Estructura de un mito literario).* Amsterdam, 1984. x, 175 pp. Paper.
17. Robert Archer: *The Pervasive Image: The Role of Analogy in the Poetry of Ausiàs March.* Amsterdam, 1985. xii, 220 pp. Paper.
18. Diana Sorensen Goodrich: *The Reader and the Text: Interpretative Strategies for Latin American Literatures.* Amsterdam, 1986. xii, 150 pp. Paper.
19. Lida Aronne-Amestoy: *Utopía, paraíso e historia: inscripciones del mito en García Márquez, Rulfo y Cortázar.* Amsterdam, 1986. xii, 167 pp. Paper.

20. Louise Mirrer-Singer: *The Language of Evaluation: A Sociolinguistic Approach to the Story of Pedro el Cruel in Ballad and Chronicle.* Amsterdam, 1986. xii, 128 pp. Paper.
21. Jo Ann Marie Recker: *"Appelle-moi 'Pierrot'": Wit and Irony in the "Lettres" of Madame de Sévigné.* Amsterdam, 1986. x, 128 pp. Paper.
22. J. H. Matthews: *André Breton: Sketch for an Early Portrait.* Amsterdam, 1986. xii, 176 pp. Paper.
23. Peter V. Conroy, Jr.: *Intimate, Intrusive, and Triumphant: Readers in the "Liaisons dangereuses."* Amsterdam, 1987. xii, 139 pp. Paper.
24. Mary Jane Stearns Schenck: *The Fabliaux: Tales of Wit and Deception.* Amsterdam, 1987. xiv, 168 pp. Paper.
25. Joan Tasker Grimbert: *"Yvain" dans le miroir: Une Poétique de la réflexion dans le "Chevalier au lion" de Chrétien de Troyes.* Amsterdam, 1988. xii, 226 pp. Cloth and paper.
26. Anne J. Cruz: *Imitación y transformación: el petrarquismo en la poesía de Boscán y Garcilaso de la Vega.* Amsterdam, 1988. x, 156 pp. Cloth and paper.
27. Alicia G. Andreu: *Modelos dialógicos en la narrativa de Benito Pérez Galdós.* Amsterdam, 1989. xvi, 126 pp. Cloth and paper.
28. Milorad R. Margitić, ed.: *Le Cid: Tragi-comédie.* By Pierre Corneille. A critical edition. Amsterdam, 1989. lxxxvi, 302 pp. Cloth and paper.
29. Stephanie A. Sieburth: *Reading "La Regenta": Duplicitous Discourse and the Entropy of Structure.* Amsterdam, 1990. viii, 127 pp. Cloth and paper.
30. Malcolm K. Read: *Visions in Exile: The Body in Spanish Literature and Linguistics: 1500-1800.* Amsterdam, 1990. xii, 211 pp. Cloth and paper.
31. María Alicia Amadei-Pulice: *Calderón y el Barroco: exaltación y engaño de los sentidos.* Amsterdam, 1990. xii, 258 pp., 33 ills. Cloth and paper.
32. Lou Charnon-Deutsch: *Gender and Representation: Women in Spanish Realist Fiction.* Amsterdam, 1990. xiv, 205 pp., 6 ills. Cloth and paper.
33. Thierry Boucquey: *Mirages de la farce: Fête des fous, Bruegel et Molière.* Amsterdam, 1991. xviii, 145 pp., 9 ills. Cloth.
34. Elżbieta Skłodowska: *La parodia en la nueva novela hispanoamericana (1960-1985).* Amsterdam, 1991. xx, 219 pp. Cloth.
35. Julie Candler Hayes: *Identity and Ideology: Diderot, Sade, and the Serious Genre.* Amsterdam, 1991. xiv, 186 pp. Cloth.
36. Aimée Israel-Pelletier: *Flaubert's Straight and Suspect Saints: The Unity of "Trois contes."* Amsterdam, 1991. xii, 165 pp. Cloth.
37. Susan Petit: *Michel Tournier's Metaphysical Fictions.* Amsterdam, 1991. xvi, 224 pp. Cloth.
38. María Cristina Quintero: *Poetry as Play: "Gongorismo" and the "Comedia."* Amsterdam, 1991. xviii, 260 pp. Cloth.
39. Michael Vincent: *Figures of the Text: Reading and Writing (in) La Fontaine.* Amsterdam, 1992. xiv, 154 pp. Cloth.